A CENTURY
OF STORIES
NEW HANOVER COUNTY PUBLIC LIBRARY
1906-2006

I Shouldn't Even Be Doing This!

I Shouldn't

‹　‹　‹　‹　‹　○　›　›　›　›　›

Even Be Doing This!

and other things that strike me as funny

Bob Newhart

HYPERION   New York

Library of Congress Cataloging-in-Publication Data

Newhart, Bob.
  I shouldn't even be doing this : and other things that strike me as funny / by Bob Newhart.—1st ed.
    p.   cm.
  ISBN 1-4013-0246-7 (hardcover)
  1. Newhart, Bob.   2. Comedians—United States—Biography.
  3. Television actors and actresses—United States—Biography   I. Title.
PN2287.N43A3   2006
792.702'8092—dc22   2006007613

Design by Fritz Metsch

FIRST EDITION

10   9   8   7   6   5   4   3   2   1

Contents

Acknowledgments

To Ginnie, my wife of forty-three years, and to my children, Rob, Tim, Jennifer, and Courtney, along with Ginnie for putting up with the vagaries of the life of a stand-up comedian, and to my grandchildren, Taylor, Maddie, Bella, Will, Caroline, Timothy, and Griffin, for all the joy and laughter they give.

To Josh Young, who gave structure to my "Stew," and Will Schwalbe, my editor at Hyperion, for his dogged determination to get a book out of me.

I Shouldn't Even
Be Doing This!

Don't Judge My Book By Its Title

I realize that most people skip the introduction and the acknowledgments. If you are one of these people, then you're not even reading this. But if you are, I want to share with you the alternative titles I had for this book.

I was told by my editor that titles sell books, so the first title I proposed was *A Slimmer You in Three Weeks*. That would've been an instant best seller because diet books sell like crazy. But my publisher's weak-kneed lawyers refused to approve the title because there were no diet tips in my book.

My next title was *Finding Mr. Right*, because dating books are also very popular. Again, the attorneys nixed this idea, this time on the grounds that the book contained no dating tips. The attorneys suggested that I find something related to comedy in some way since I am a comedian.

I came up with *The Fat Lady in the Pink Dress Wants a White Wine*. This comes from the parties we've had at our house when my kids helped serve the grown-ups. I'd ask my son to go and see what Mrs. Petersen would like to drink. He'd come back and say, "The fat lady in the pink dress wants a white wine."

Besides being a catchy phrase, I thought this would make a nice title for a book written by a comedian. When you mature, you realize you can't say something like that in polite company. But comedians don't mature. For some reason, comedians are still children. The social skills somehow never reach us, so we say exactly what we think without weighing the results. But as a title, it sounded too much like a book written by a bartender.

You Didn't Let Me Finish was a candidate because it neatly sums up Hollywood. I first heard the phrase in a story about Harry Crane, a comedy writer who worked for Dean Martin. Harry was sent by Greg Garrison, who produced *The Dean Martin Show*, to check out a lounge singer that they were thinking of booking on the show. The singer, it turned out, was Mama Cass, back when she was known as Cass Elliot.

Harry completed the trip and reported back to Garrison: "This immense woman walks out on the stage in a muumuu and it's stained," he said. "It's not even clean. She had perspiration dripping down both armpits, and she cannot sing. She can't carry a note."

Garrison interrupted, "Dean loves her." To which Crane said, "You didn't let me finish."

Deciding that was too Hollywood, I toyed with *Which One Would You Like to Hear Again?* This phrase was my sole line of defense as a naïve and neophyte stand-up.

It was my very first stand-up gig, and I was the opening act at the Tidelands Motor Inn in Houston. I performed the only three routines I had, "Abe Lincoln vs. Madison Avenue," "The Driving Instructor," and "The Cruise of the U.S.S. *Codfish*." The audience was particularly responsive one night, and they gave me a lengthy applause. As I left the stage, I walked by the maître d'.

"Go back out there. They want to hear more," he said.

"That's all I have," I explained.

I reluctantly walked back onstage. The applause died down, and I asked them, "Which one would you like to hear again?"

In considering phrases that have stuck with me over the years, I recalled a story that Art Linkletter used to tell in his routine on how kids say the darnedest things. In one bit, there was a boy who was off by himself brooding in a corner while all the other kids were laughing and enjoying themselves. Art went over to the boy and attempted to comfort him.

"Is something wrong?" Art asked.

"Yeah, my dog died this week," the boy said.

"Well," Art said, "your dog went to heaven and when you go to heaven you will see your dog again so don't be too unhappy."

The boy looked at Art quizzically. "What does God want with a dead dog?" Another example of the logic of children.

And then there's the title I settled on: *I Shouldn't Even Be Doing This!*

That's from a gag about a guy who is having an affair with his boss's wife. They are making mad, passionate love, and she says, "Kiss me! Kiss me!"

He looks at her very seriously and replies, "I shouldn't even be doing *this*!"

That disproportionate side of life ties nicely to my career. I became a comedian by way of accounting. I recorded several comedy albums, three with *The Button-Down Mind* in the title. I starred in several television series, all of which have my name in the title: *The Bob Newhart Show*, *The Bob Newhart Show* (again), *Newhart*, *Bob*, and *George and Leo* (a bit of a stretch but it uses my given name, George Robert Newhart). I acted in several movies that didn't have my name in the title, including *Hell Is for Heroes*, *Catch-22*, and *Elf*, and I guest starred on *ER* and *Desperate Housewives*. All the while, I've been married to the same woman for forty-three years, had four children, played countless rounds of golf, and met some very interesting people.

However, it didn't take me long to realize that I couldn't write a traditional memoir. A memoir is a weighty tome. Former presidents and the Marquis de Sade write memoirs; Bob Newhart doesn't write a memoir. So I proposed that we call it a roman à clef and leave it at that. Again, my weak-kneed lawyers objected.

But the biggest problem of all came when I was halfway finished with the book. I began to get nervous because deep in the process of writing a book about myself, I didn't have one of the primary ingredients. I wasn't feeling cathartic. I've read enough of these kinds of books and seen enough authors promote them on talk shows to know that they are always cathartic. So I sent the book to a specialist in recognizing catharsis and asked him if what he read could be considered cathartic.

"No, it's self-pity," he said. "But I like the title."

CHAPTER ONE

Comedians See Life
Through a Different Lens

Most comedians are committable. People say I'm the most normal of all comedians—and I'm still certifiable.

Larry Gelbart once said that comedians look at life through a different lens. Comedians by nature are observers of people. Even if a comedian is on vacation and he sees something funny on the beach, he'll say to himself, "I have to remember that because I may need it someday."

When I was a child, I remember watching a garbage truck with the name "Neal Norlag" on the side. Subconsciously, I filed the name away for later use. *Remember Neal Norlag.*

Comedians are innately programmed to pick up oddities like mispronounced words, upside-down books on a shelf, and generally undetectable mistakes in everyday life.

Recently, for instance, I've noticed on the cable news channels that the guy who writes the news crawl along the bottom of the screen can't type. Clearly, there is no one watching him and saying, "Gary, what's wrong with you?"

These aren't glaring errors, but they certainly stand out to me. One day last summer, a typically misspelled news bulletin announced: "In the Mideast, peace talks are underway between the Palestinians and the Israelis and there is the possibility that Egypt may play a roll"—as opposed to a "role."

Stranger still, I came across a solemn news item in the newspaper about an assassination in Afghanistan. A minister was killed. I read further. It turned out that he was the minister of tourism. Now, how busy can Afghanistan's minister of tourism possibly be? You don't picture a young honeymooning couple saying, "Enough of the bickering. Let's flip a coin: It's Paris or Kabul."

Maybe I am the only one who notices.

I think it was Jack Benny who once said, "A comic says funny things, but a comedian says things funny." I guess I'd fall into that latter grouping.

•

Many comedians would probably agree that you start off doing someone else while your own voice evolves. You start out as an imitator because hiding behind success is easier than finding it. Richard Pryor started out doing Bill Cosby and then came into his own. For me, the models were Mike and Elaine, Bob and Ray, and, of course, Benny.

When I first performed, I didn't study all the working comedians and say, "There is nobody stammering out there.... What a great opportunity." In interviews throughout my career, I've often been asked if my stammer was natural. My stock response: "Have you been listening to my answers?"

Truly, that's . . . the . . . way I talk.

When I was doing *The Bob Newhart Show*, one of the producers pulled me aside and said that the shows were running a little long. He wondered if I could cut down the time of my speeches by reducing my stammering. "No," I told him. "That stammer bought me a house in Beverly Hills."

Stammering is different than stuttering. Stutterers have trouble with the letters, while stammerers trip over entire parts of a sentence. We stammerers generally think of ourselves as very bright. My own private theory is that stammerers have so many ideas swirling around their brains at once that they can't get them all out, though I haven't found any scientific evidence to back that up.

There are exceptions to the imitation rule. I remember watching a show on TV from the Improv in New York one night in the eighties. One young comedian after another came onstage. I'd say to myself, "Okay, he's doing Seinfeld. He's doing Benny." Then Norm MacDonald appeared. He wasn't doing anyone. He was doing himself, which made him stand out.

Norm later wrote a sketch for me when I hosted *Saturday Night Live*. I played a supervisor at the post office who had to discipline a disgruntled worker regarding his appearance. Gingerly I instructed Norm's beatnik character: "There is a uniform that you have to wear. Again, let me assure you that this is coming from the guys upstairs and I'm just relaying it to you. It's strictly procedure. I personally have nothing against combat fatigues, but it's just that the guys upstairs . . ."

Long before I started performing my own routines on-stage, I loved watching comedians on television. I'd hear a joke and then ask myself why it got a laugh. What made it work? Why did he choose that particular word? In the fifties, I watched George Gobel. He wasn't doing "Take My Wife, Please." He would just tell these neat little stories, like about how his wife, spooky ole Alice, came up to him the other day. It was a softer, less aggressive brand of comedy. Later I saw Bob and Ray performing similar routines. I thought to myself, you can be successful without having to be as broad as some of the comedians were in the early years.

That was the first inkling I had that maybe I could make it as a comedic storyteller.

But it wasn't all positive reinforcement. Early in my career, I saw Jonathan Winters perform in a comedy club in Chicago. He was hilarious. Each joke was funnier than the one before it. I was totally discouraged. I thought to myself, why bother? There's no way you can be as funny as Jonathan Winters.

I gathered my wits and decided that being No. 2 wouldn't be so bad.

The greatest comedian I've ever seen is Jack Benny. He wasn't afraid of the silences. Once Benny was following the Will Maston Trio with Sammy Davis Jr. They absolutely killed. The audience was still applauding for them when Benny walked onstage. He complimented them and then started his routine.

"In the afternoon, I like to have some tea. I go in the coffee shop, around four o'clock or four-fifteen." Pause. "More like four-thirty." (Terrifically unnecessary information, by the way.) Pause. "So I went into the coffee shop.... I did a movie with an English actor whose name I couldn't remember ... he was in the coffee shop, but I couldn't remember his name ..."

Here Benny stopped for what seemed like an eternity. "I'm sorry," he said, breaking the silence. "I promised Sammy Davis Jr. that he could do another number. Let's hear another number from him."

Everyone dutifully applauded, and Sammy reappeared onstage. He performed "Birth of the Blues," and destroyed the audience again. Benny returned to the stage, himself applauding, and watched Sammy and the band walk off. When the applause finally died down, Benny said, "Nevil. That was his name ... Nevil."

Trust me, you don't do that unless you know it will play.

•

The interesting thing I discovered about my material was that once I convince the audience to accept the premise, then everything that follows is logical. My routine "Defusing the Bomb," for instance, is about a small-town patrolman named Willard Hackmeister who finds a live mortar shell on the beach and calls headquarters to ask how to proceed. If you accept the fact that he's in a small town that doesn't have the equipment necessary to defuse a bomb, everything that follows is logical.

Take my two favorite lines:

"Willard," his captain says over the phone, "if this thing goes off, it's me they are going to want to talk to."

Later, the captain adds: "Willard, if we can save one human life ... that's the way you feel about it, too."

For some routines like "King Kong," the jump is a tad bigger. If you accept the premise that King Kong really existed and was this huge ape who came to New York, that it could have been the first night on the job for this new security guard at the Empire State Building, and that a large ape climbing the building wouldn't have been covered in the guard's week-long orientation and training program or mentioned in any of the manuals and therefore would cause the guard to reluctantly call his supervisor, then everything else that follows is logical.

"King Kong" is a routine that came to me full-born. It happened when I was living in New York doing the television show *The Entertainers* with Carol Burnett. My wife, Ginnie, and I were having dinner with Carol and her husband, Joe Hamilton, at the Top of the Sixes restaurant, which had a panoramic view of Manhattan. I was talking about jobs that I held before I became a stand-up. From my seat I could see the Empire State Building out the window all lit up. I made a connection between these two seemingly opposite thoughts, and *boom!* The whole routine just came full-blown. Like this:

Hello, Mr. Nelson. This is Sam Hennessy, the new guard. Sir, I hate to bother you at home like this on my first night, but, uh, something's come up and it's not covered in the guard's manual. . . . Yeah, I looked in the index, yes, sir. I looked under unauthorized personnel and people without passes and apes and apes' toes. . . . Apes and apes' toes, yes, sir. There's an ape's toe sticking through the window, sir. . . . See, this isn't your standard ape, sir. He's between eighteen and nineteen stories high, depending on whether there is a thirteenth floor or not. . . . Sir, I'm sure there's a

*rule against apes shaking the building. . . . There is, yes, sir.
So I yelled at his feet. I said, "Shoo, ape," and "I'm sorry
but you are going to have to leave." . . . I know how you like
the new men to think on their feet, so I went to the broom
closet and I got out a broom without signing out a requisi-
tion on it. . . . I will tomorrow, yes sir. . . . And I started hitting him on the toes with it. It didn't bother him much. . . .
See, there are these planes and they are flying around
him . . . and they are shooting at him and they only seem to
be bothering him a little bit, so I figured I wasn't doing too
much good with a broom. Did I try swatting him in the
face with it? Well, I was going to take the elevator up to his
head, but my jurisdiction only extends to his navel. You
don't care what I do . . . just get the ape off the building.
This may complicate things a little—he's carrying a
woman in his hand, sir. . . . No, I don't think she works in
the building, no, sir. . . . As he passed by my floor . . . she has
a kind of negligee on, so I doubt very much she's one of the
cleaning women. Well, sir, the first thing I did was I filled
out a report on it. Well, I don't want to give the building a
bad name either, sir, but I doubt very much if we can cover
it up, sir. The planes are shooting at him, and people are
going to come to work in the morning and some of them
are going to notice the ape in the street and the broken window, and they will start putting two and two together. I
think we're safe on that score, sir. I doubt very much if he
signed the book downstairs. You don't care what I do . . . just
get the ape off the building. Well, I came up with one idea.
I thought maybe I could smear the Chrysler Building with
bananas . . .*

•

One problem with being a stand-up is that other people feel incumbent to show you that they have a sense of humor. It's like telling a plumber who is working on your house that you once fixed the kitchen sink. The subtext is that you know what it's like.

Not long ago, my dentist, who is a woman, told me a story about her girlfriend, who is a comedienne. Her girlfriend is single so the dentist fixed her up with a lawyer. She gave the lawyer the comedienne's phone number. He called and they talked for a while. Days later, the dentist asked her friend if the two had gone out yet.

"No," the comedienne said. "He's an amateur."

Usually when people tell me jokes, they tell the dirtiest jokes imaginable. They'll preface the joke by telling me that I will have to clean this up a little bit if I want to use it in my act. Especially me, Mr. PG.

"I've got a great joke, but in the punch line there is a bad word," the guy will say to me. "Can I tell you the joke even though the punch line is a little off-center?"

"Sure, let's hear it," I'll say.

And it turns out the very first line is R-rated.

Personally, I've never done an outrageously raunchy joke onstage. I just don't feel comfortable with shock for shock's sake. I've found there is a level that you set for yourself and one that the audience sets for you. You can approach that level, but you can't penetrate it because then your routine becomes unacceptable. The trick is to come as close to that line as you can. That's where the tension is.

For example, I'll say something slightly subversive like,

"Doctors say that Viagra doesn't cause blindness." I'll pause, and then I'll walk into the microphone, which results in a few relieved chuckles.

Viagra may be the word that causes people to become a little uptight because they aren't sure what's coming next. I was at dinner with Tim Conway and the subject came up. Tim said, "They say if you have an erection that lasts more than four hours, call your doctor. Hey, if I have an erection that lasts for more than four hours, I'm calling everybody I know."

Truthfully, there's no subject I've ruled out completely. If I have a really killer joke, everything is subject to negotiation. My wife always says, "If they found out what your sense of humor is really like, no one would show up. You have this dark side."

It's somewhat true. In real life, I tend to find humor in the macabre. I love portraying the totally insensitive person. There are people out there who are totally insensitive to human feelings. These jokes are my private stock. They're just for me and my family and friends to enjoy, like a family winery that saves a rare vintage for its own holiday table.

Most of the jokes are in good fun. One time I was out to dinner with my four children, and my youngest daughter, Courtney, complained when I ordered veal. She listed all the cruel and inhumane ways in which calves were treated before being slaughtered.

At our next family dinner, I secretly submitted my own personal list of specials to the maître d'. With his French accent, he began: "Tonight, we have a lovely baby harp seal in a nice white wine sauce. My favorite is the tender rare condor sautéed with lemon and capers . . ." After he worked his way down a virtual list of endangered species, Courtney was truly mortified—until she saw a big grin form on my face.

•

Nearly all comedians enjoy a camaraderie with their brethren. I liken it to the friend of mine who once dated Elizabeth Taylor. My friend was the most unlikely guy to date Liz Taylor, but they somehow ended up getting engaged. When they broke up before marrying, he was despondent. I said to him, "Look at it this way: You are like an astronaut. There are only about twenty other guys you can talk to who know what you are talking about."

This made him feel much better.

Comedians can only discuss certain things with other comedians, because if you have never done stand-up, you don't know what it's like. You don't know the feel of an audience. I'll be talking to my friend Don Rickles and I'll say, "I had this audience and they were just dead. You know what I mean?" And he'll say, "Yeah, I had one like that in Cleveland in ninety-one."

Nobody else would know what that feeling is like, and that forms a bond that extends beyond who knows whom. In 1960, I was playing a club called Freddie's in Minneapolis. Freddie's was only the sixth club I played as a professional stand-up, so I remember it well. It was a long, thin room that held 400 and had a bar behind the stage. The people who could see my face were paying more than those watching the back of my head. The bartenders were real pros. They knew each comic's routine and timed the ringing up of their sales to the punch line so laughter would drown out the cash register.

Late one morning during my run at Freddie's, I was in my hotel room and I got a call from Dick Martin, whom I had never met. He was also in Minneapolis; Rowan and Martin were appearing in the Flame Room at the Radisson. He told me that he was playing golf that afternoon at Interlochen, a first-rate course where it's hard to get a tee time, and he invited me to join his foursome. I accepted.

For stand-ups, it's perfectly acceptable to call one another even though you haven't met. The feeling is, I don't know you, but you are another stand-up. You've been through the wars, fought back the hecklers, and lived to tell another joke.

Stand-up comedy is not for the faint of heart or small of ego. Basically, a comedian is introduced to a paying audience. He (or she) walks out on the stage. The subtext is that he (or she) is going to make the audience laugh for an hour and a half. That's a pretty conceited thing to say.

In nightclubs, you are performing, as the catchphrase goes, without a net. Singers can hide behind a song, with excuses like "I never cared for that arrangement" or "those are the dumbest lyrics." Sinatra once said about *Strangers in the Night* that if you liked that song, you'd like orange yogurt. He thought it was stupid, yet he sang it because people wanted to hear it.

As a stand-up, if the audience doesn't laugh, they're saying, "You're not funny." And that's personal.

I've never thought of myself as a gambler, but I guess I am. Every night I perform, there is that risk: Will it or will it not work? When it works, I get an adrenaline rush. When it doesn't, there's such a terrible low that I've even blamed my partner. Never mind that it's a telephone.

•

Just in case you ever run into one in the real world, here are a few dirty little secrets about comedians:

Comedians are sadistic.

There's an old joke that perfectly illustrates how comedians see themselves. One comedian—an opening act, not a headliner—is talking to another comedian. "Over the last couple of weeks, it has been weird," he says. "I'm opening for Steve and Eydie. I finish and walk offstage, and they walk on. But the people were still applauding for me, so Steve and Eydie call me back. A week later, I'm opening for Tony Bennett and the same thing happens. I finish, people are applauding, and Tony calls me back onstage for an encore. But then last Thursday, I'm at this club and I died."

"Yeah," says the other comedian. "I heard about that."

Comedians are self-absorbed.

Again, an illustrative story. A fair-to-mid-level comedian is onstage at a nothing kind of place. He does his show to polite applause and walks offstage. A woman comes backstage to tell him how much the show meant to her.

"I lost my husband six months ago," she begins. "I loved him very much. We had spent our whole lives together. I was walking by and I saw your name and I thought to myself, 'Gee, I'd like to laugh. That's what I need, a good laugh because I've been in mourning for six months.' And I came in, and it's the first time I've laughed in six months. If there is anything I can do, I don't know how to repay you. If there is anything I can do, any sexual favor you would like . . ."

The comedian interrupts her. "Did you see the first show or the second show?"

Comedians have multiple personalities.

Buddy Hackett was working on his famous Chinese-waiter routine—the one where he puts a rubber band around his eyes to force them into slits and then lectures the diner, "You get one from column A and one from column B. . . . No, those two are from column A . . . you only get one from column A." He came home one night during the time that the routine was still in the developmental stage and said to his wife, Sherry, "Do you know what he said tonight . . . ?"

Comedians have a perverse sense of humor.

I once opened a show in Vegas at the Frontier Hotel by telling the backstage announcer to give me a long, drawn out buildup, and then stop the hydraulic stage short. "Ladies and gentlemen . . . drumroll . . . The Frontier Hotel . . . drumroll . . . takes great pride in presenting . . . drumroll . . . *Bobbbbb Newhart!*" With that, the back half of the stage slowly rose, revealing my head and chest, and there it stopped. I climbed up onto the stage—and nothing. No reaction at all from the audience.

I still think it was a hilarious gag.

Comedians can bury a joke just like your uncle.

Ed Sullivan once had Jack Jones on his show as an entertainer. After Jack had finished singing, Ed called him back on stage, as he did from time to time. Jack returned and Ed asked, "Jack, didn't your father used to be Alan Jones?" Jack replied: "He still is."

That was on the afternoon show. The audience roared. Ed told Jack they would repeat the exchange that night because the audience thought it was so funny. After Jack sang his two songs for the second show, Ed called him over and asked, "Jack, is your father still alive?" Jack gave Ed a blank stare . . . and there was total silence from the audience.

Comedians can teach you something.

Many jokes are like adult Aesop's fables. Take Danny Thomas's classic "jack story."

Danny used to do a routine in which a guy's car gets a flat tire. The guy has a spare but no jack, so he has to walk to the nearest garage to rent a jack. The guy thinks out loud, "I have to rent a jack. What do they want for a jack? Twenty bucks? I've got to have the jack to fix the flat, and the garage attendant knows I've got to have the jack."

The guy keeps walking. "He could ask for fifty bucks, and I'm going to have to pay it. . . . Actually, he could ask for a hundred bucks if he really wanted to. . . . My god, he could ask for five hundred for the jack."

Finally, when the guy reaches the garage, he says to the attendant, "You can take that five-hundred-dollar jack and shove it up your ass."

For those of you who missed the point: Slow down, take a breath, and have a conversation.

Some comedians cannot tell a joke.

Everyone is probably familiar with the story about the new guy in prison on death row. The first day he's locked up, another inmate yells out, "Twenty-four!" Everyone on death row breaks up laughing. A little time goes by and another prisoner shouts, "Seventeen!" Again, everyone cracks up. The new guy asks another inmate, "What is that?" The inmate says, "They are telling jokes. We all know the joke, so they just give the number." The new guy says, "Let me try. Twenty-nine!" Nothing happens. The inmate says, "See, some people can tell jokes and some people can't."

Many good comedians can't remember the jokes, so they just do punch lines. If someone gives me the punch line, I can generally build backward to the joke. Dick Martin and Don Rickles can't remember jokes, so all we do is punch lines.

"Why, is one missing?"

The story: "Did you take a shower?"

Or: "I'll get the half that eats."

The story: "I'm dating this girl and she works for a magician. Every night, he saws her in half. With my luck, I'll get the half that eats."

All comedians are thin-skinned.

So please do not write to me or the publisher if you don't like this book.

On the other hand, ventriloquists are downright crazy.

Dick Martin knew a ventriloquist named Pat Patrick who committed suicide by throwing himself from a plane. Pat Patrick left a note that read, "The dummy pushed me."

hot in the summer to walk around with any pretenses. You've got to be as real and solid as one of those bone-in rib eyes served at Gibsons Steakhouse. It's a city where you say what you mean, mean what you say, and, most importantly, where you must be able to back up what you say. All in all, this makes it a great place for comedians to sharpen their acts.

There is a long list of comedians and actors who came out of the Second City theater. The tradition began with Alan Arkin and Barbara Harris, and grew exponentially with John Belushi, Bill Murray, Dan Aykroyd, John Candy, Chris Farley, Gilda Radner, and Martin Short, to name a few. This improvisational comedy theater is also responsible for reminding the world about the Second City moniker, a phrase coined in a series of derisive *New Yorker* magazine articles by A. J. Liebling

In Chicago, there truly is a Second City mentality, a cautionary "don't think you're New York just because you have big stuff in your city." Consider that the Sears Tower was erected in 1974 as the tallest building in the world at 110 stories and 1,450 feet. Why? Because Sears needed eight more floors of office space than the Empire State Building? No, it was simply to have the tallest building in the world and be ahead of New York.

To this day, I maintain that you can't fool Chicago audiences. People in other cities laugh at what they think they should laugh at, but people in Chicago only laugh when something is funny. That's why there's such a long list of comedians who were toughened up and found success there, including Mike and Elaine, Shecky Greene,

CHAPTER TWO

Growing Up in the Windy City

Chicago is a satirical city. I know this for a fact because I grew up there.

Take its nickname: the windy city. Most people believe its derivation comes from the wind whipping off Lake Michigan and between the skyscrapers. While there is what's locally known as the "lake effect," Chicago is not considered by meteorologists to be a particularly windy city. Once we were in Chicago filming some stock footage for *The Bob Newhart Show*, and we had to rent a wind machine to blow my hat off.

There's much more evidence to suggest that the nickname metaphorically refers to the long history of blustery politicians and the excessive boasting of early Chicagoans about their rapidly growing metropolis. Though it became a term of pride, the nickname was probably given to the city by its urban rivals.

Whether blustery in words or weather, there's no putting on airs in Chicago. It's too cold in the winter and too

Mort Sahl, Jonathan Winters, Shelley Berman, and, of course, Bob Newhart.

•

Tim Conway, a dear friend of mine, tells a story about growing up in Chagrin Falls, Ohio. His father, who wasn't handy at all around the house, decided that he could install a doorbell. He completed the task, but there was a slight problem. The doorbell rang all the time except when someone actually pushed it, at which point Tim's father would say, "I'll get it."

Given this childhood, Tim could only have become a comedian.

I'll try to describe my childhood and let you decide if this is the stuff of which comedians are made.

Overall, I would say that my childhood was neither more nor less funny than the childhoods of most people I know. I was born in Oak Park Hospital, but I grew up across the town line in Austin on the West Side of Chicago. I used to say that I lived in Oak Park because it was more posh than Austin. Ernest Hemingway grew up there, and Edgar Rice Burroughs wrote twenty-two Tarzan novels while living in Oak Park. Even the founder of Austin, Henry Austin, lived in Oak Park.

I always thought we were from an upper-middle-class family until I met an upper-middle-class family and realized that we weren't. The rich people were easy to spot because they all had suntans in the wintertime. Bronzed skin in February was a status symbol in Chicago. It meant that you had vacationed in Florida over Christmas. My family didn't have much money so we didn't go to Florida. If we went on vacation, it was to Wisconsin.

My father, George, worked for a plumbing and heating contractor, and my mother, Pauline, was a homemaker. I was the second of four children, and the only boy. My sisters, Mary Joan, Pauline, and Ginny, were all very smart. Suffice it to say, I tried to get my report card home before my sisters because I knew that once theirs arrived, mine wouldn't look so good.

My sisters and I were raised Catholic and educated in Catholic schools. A religious education was important to my parents. I lived about eight blocks from Fenwick High School, but I rode the streetcar forty-five minutes to St. Ignatius. What I remember most about St. Ignatius is that it was all boys. This made for some ambiguous theater when we put on plays because the girls' parts were all played by boys. The love interests in the plays left a lot to be desired.

However, like most kids, I didn't pay much attention in church, and I only took communion because I was always hungry. Until I was an adult, I thought that St. Christopher was the patron saint of magnetic feet because you stuck him on the dashboard and he wouldn't move.

All religions basically are saying one thing, and that is: "Be nice to each other." My friends who are Jewish comedians always seemed to have a leg up because they could use Yiddish words like schmuck or putz in their acts, and talk about growing up Jewish. Our family never used Irish or German words; we just spoke plain English, which is not exactly fodder for a comedian's act.

Now, I can't be judgmental because I didn't go through

the Depression and my father did. I don't know what that does to someone, but it affected him. I know that about two years after my father and mother were married, he took a job with American Standard, which manufactures plumbing supplies. In accounting, there are two kinds of book entries: LiFo (Last in, First out) and FiFo (First in, First out). Unfortunately, he was with a FiFo company, and when the Depression hit, he lost his job.

When I was growing up, most of the time my father would come home from work around five o'clock and take a nap. In high school and college, I always worked, so I would get home around 6:30 P.M. My sisters had their own schedules. Sometimes the family would have dinner together, sometimes not. Around eight, my father would go to "Toppers," his favorite hangout. He would come home around 12:30 A.M. More often than not, this was a typical day in my father's life.

I really didn't get much recognition from my father. I don't think it scarred me for life; it's just the way it was. The more I read, the more I think that's just the way fathers were at the time. I was a little bit like the son in the novel *The Kite Runner*, who was always trying to gain his father's attention and affection but never succeeded. When I read the book, their relationship struck a responsive chord.

My mother's father, whose name was Danny Burns, had some money. He owned an apartment building at 59 North Menard Street, where my parents lived rent-free for a while. My father owned a car that he parked out back, but he didn't drive it because he couldn't afford the gasoline.

Being kids, we used to play in the car. We would fill up the gas tank with sand. The day came when my father had saved enough money to buy gas and he discovered what we had done. Predictably, he went ballistic. My mother interceded. She said, "If you ever lay a hand on the kids, I'll kill you." And she meant it.

Years later, in 1989, my family in Chicago was at a Christmas gathering. My sister M.J. was seated next to my mother. Mom's memory was beginning to fade. My mother said, "Is Dad with us?" M.J. said, "No, Mom, Dad died a few months ago." Mom said, "There were times I could have killed him." Then there was a pause and Mom said, "I didn't, did I?" with a laugh.

Eventually we moved from the apartment building into a duplex at 26 North Mason Street. The story I heard was that my grandfather had taken out bonds for the apartment building but defaulted on them because the tenants couldn't pay their rent. Soon he sold his half of the duplex and moved in with us upstairs. My grandfather took my bedroom, and I slept in the dining room. That's when I truly realized we weren't middle class.

When my grandfather died, I got my bedroom back. Then my grandmother on my father's side, Emma O'Connor-Newhart, moved in with us, and I was back in the dining room.

No matter where we lived, I remember that the Kentucky Derby was always a big event in our house. At the time, I thought it was part of our heritage, but there may have been more to it. I knew that my mother's parents, the Burnses, had moved to Chicago from Maysville, Kentucky, so I assumed there was a natural interest in the race because of that.

So you can take from my childhood whatever you want and decide that's why I became a comedian, but I don't like to analyze my comedy on that basis. Oh, yeah . . . there is one more piece of information from my childhood to factor in: I was addicted to Pepsi.

•

The real personality test for Chicagoans is whether they are Cubs fans or White Sox fans. For years, the two baseball teams have divided the town. The Cubs play on the North Side in homey, ivy-covered Wrigley Field, while the Sox play on the South Side in a stone fortress now called U.S. Cellular Field. The dividing line for fans is at Madison Street, which literally divides the North Side of the city from the South. We lived on the West Side, so we could go either way.

My mom was a Cubs fan and so was I. She and a friend often took me to games when I was young. My dad was a Sox fan. I never went to Sox games.

Listening on the radio to a typical Sox game, I would hear that Nellie Fox would walk. Then the next batter, Luis Aparicio, would bunt, and Nellie Fox would run to second. Next, Minnie Minoso would hit a fly ball, and Fox would go to third. Finally, somebody would single and Fox would score. It was dull.

But the Cubs were exciting. Bill Nicholson could hit a homer at any time and clear the bases. I can still name the lineup from the 1945 Cubs, the last team to win the pennant. They were: Phil Cavarretta at first base, Don John-son at second, Roy Hughes at shortstop, Stan Hack at third, Mickey Livingston behind the plate, Hank Borowy on the mound, and Peanuts Lowrey, Andy Pafko, and Nicholson in the outfield. Really, that was from memory!

Until 2005, when the Sox won the World Series, both Chicago teams had underachievement in common. The Cubs, known affectionately as the "lovable losers," had not won the series since 1908, and the Sox hadn't won since 1917. While the White Sox have forever been plagued by the "Black Sox" scandal of 1919, in which several players took bribes from gamblers and threw the World Series, the Cubs are famous for the curse that happened in 1945—the last time they made it to the World Series.

As legend has it, a bar owner named Billy Sianis brought his pet goat to game four of the 1945 World Series and was ejected on orders of owner P. K. Wrigley midway through the game because the goat smelled. Sianis, who owned the Billy Goat Tavern, hexed the Cubs, declaring that they would never win the World Series as long as the goat was not allowed at Wrigley Field.

Over the years, every time the Cubs have gotten close to winning the pennant and advancing to the World Series, something bizarre has snatched it away and talk of the curse is renewed. When I lived in Chicago, I was never fa-miliar with the curse. I was just perennially disappointed.

•

My dad was a good bowler. Despite the fact that the eight-lane Austin-Madison bowling alley was a half a block from where we lived and the fact that I worked there as a pin spotter in high school, he always bowled at the sixteen-lane Cinderella bowling alley.

For two years, I was a pin spotter at Austin-Madison Bowling Alley from 6:30 P.M. until 10:30 P.M. every night. These were the days before the automatic resetting machines at bowling alleys, and the pin spotter's job was to manually replace the pins after each frame.

Pin spotting required dexterity. After placing the pins down in one alley, you would stand in the adjacent alley while the bowlers used the first alley. For four hours, you alternated resetting the pins in those two alleys. It was also a somewhat dangerous job. Every now and then, a pin called a chaser would fly from one alley into the next and whiz around your feet, hitting the sides and the back of the area where you were standing.

If a guy threw a chaser, I often sent him a subtle message.

The first measure of revenge was to take the five pin (the middle pin in the triangle of ten pins) and offset it just a little bit. It was almost imperceptible, but just enough so that if he threw a perfect ball into the 1-3 pocket, he ended up with a split and not a strike. A good bowler would get the message: Don't throw a chaser.

The other message you could send was lamely rolling the ball up the ball return so that it wouldn't make it up and over the hump. The ball would then roll back down and come to rest in the middle of the lane, and the guy would have to walk down the gutter to retrieve it.

The women's leagues were usually easier than the men's. Because women didn't generally throw with the power of men, I would sit on the bench at the end of the lane where the women were bowling, hold my feet up, and put my hand over a certain place that I didn't want to be hit by a bowling ball.

However, I remember picking up the pins once for a woman who didn't know the basic etiquette of bowling. As I started placing the few pins that this woman knocked down on the rack, I heard a *"cudump, cudump, cudump..."* Instinctively, I knew that the ball was coming right for me. Thankfully, she was so bad that she rolled the ball on the holes, allowing me to hear it. Had she thrown a spinner, I would've been a goner.

My colleagues were two grown men, a guy named Branch who was attending barber school, and an Eastern European who spoke no English. Branch and I would talk across the lanes by yelling at each other over the sound of clanking pins. I remember him loudly telling me about his barber-school final exam, in which he had to lather a balloon with shaving cream and shave the balloon without popping it. I never found out if he passed.

Pin spotting paid ten cents per round, earning me about six dollars for the night. After work, I would stick around and bowl a few games. The problem with this was that the alley charged one dollar a game and had no employee discount, so I ended up bowling away half my nightly wages.

I was a decent bowler. I threw what was called a semi-spinner, which doesn't have the driving power of a full-roller. The full-roller bores through the pins to bowl a strike, while the semi-spinner jumbles them. I did that for years and carried a 170 average. Then one day, I threw my semi-spinner, and it dawned on me that I was never going to get any better.

So after devoting all that time to spotting pins, missing prime TV, and squandering half my earnings to boot, I quit bowling.

•

I did mine some comedic material from my everyday childhood world. My street was near the end of the suburban Chicago Transit Authority bus line. From around the time I was five years old, I watched the buses drive up our street, and then turn around and head back to town.

One day I began to wonder what kind of school bus drivers attended. Like baseball players, I reasoned, if there were good bus drivers, then there must be great bus drivers. This led to my imagining a school for bus drivers because they couldn't innately know what to do—or how to treat people so rudely.

In a routine that I wrote just before moving away from Chicago titled "Bus Driver's School," I take the audience to that school. As we enter the school, there is a course in progress to train bus drivers:

Here is the situation, Johnson. You have just pulled into a stop. You have discharged your passengers and out of your mirror, you notice this old woman running for a bus. Let's see how Johnson handles it.... Hold it, hold it. You are pulling out much too fast, Johnson. See, she gave up about halfway down the block. What you want to do is kind of gradually ease out so they are always holding out hope that they will catch the bus. One thing you want to watch out for, a lot of these old women will run at three-quarters speed. Then they'll put on a final burst and they'll catch up with the bus.

Graham, you want to try now. Okay, let's see how Graham

handles this situation. All right, did you all see how he slammed the door right in her face that time? That's known as your perfect pullout.... It wasn't part of your problem, but I want to compliment you on it: You blocked both lanes pulling in.

Mrs. Selkirk, I think we'll take situation thirteen. You want to get in the Chevrolet. Drivers, you will be driving and there will be a student driver. Let's see how Johnson goes about handling this situation.... That was fine, very good. Could you all see what he did? He gets back about ten to fifteen car lengths, gets it up to around sixty miles per hour, and then he gets right behind her ... bang! He slams on his brakes and hits the horn at the same time. Did you all see how the car went out of control there? The minute she dove for the floorboard, it just swerved into the light pole.

Mrs. Selkirk, you be the woman with the package.... Granted, you drivers can't be expected to know this. It is going to take time and lots of practice.... Mrs. Selkirk, fumble for your change.... Start heading for the back of the bus.... Johnson, hit your accelerator, then the brake, hit the accelerator again, now your brake. Did you see how she spun all the way to the front of the bus? Don't get discouraged. Within five to six months, you'll have all of them spinning. Just remember, accelerator, brake, accelerator, brake.

Finally, for homework tonight, you are going to study the mispronunciation of street names.

If none of that is funny to you, it may be because you've never seen a friendly neighbor in a fedora cursed by a bus driver for not getting off fast enough who then shouts back at the bus driver: "Same to you, fella!"

CHAPTER THREE

I Almost Had a Real Career

I heard my name being called out for the third time. It had already been called out for best new artist and best comedy performance. This time was for album of the year, beating out Harry Belafonte and Frank Sinatra. As I was walking up to receive my Grammy, I thought to myself, maybe now Dad will notice me.

But I'm getting ahead of myself.

Being a comedian means you are anti-authority or sub-versive at heart. You are looking to expose the loopholes in the system, sometimes to make things easier and other times just because they're there. Looking back at my life and career, I realize I was always anti-authority at heart. It just took me a while to realize it.

After making it through the Catholic grade school St. Catherine of Siena, the Catholic high school St. Ignatius, and the Catholic college Loyola University, I enrolled in Loyola's law school, which was also affiliated with the Catholic Church. I had my undergraduate degree in management (heavy on accounting classes), and I was on a career path to become a lawyer.

What drew me to the law? I'm not exactly sure, though I was a voracious reader of the works of Robert Benchley, and at least on a subconscious level, one of Benchley's essays influenced me to go to law school. It was about a Walter Mitty–type character who was a trial lawyer. This attorney made an absolute fool out of the opposing counsel to the point where the jury was applauding and even the judge was enjoying the show.

While attending law school, I worked as a law clerk in the afternoons for a firm run by three brothers. Their firm handled wage garnishments. My job involved going to a local factory, finding the guy who owed money, and bringing him back to the law office in a taxi so he could sign the papers to have his wages garnished. Even for a lawyer, it was a creepy way to make a living.

One day, one of the brothers asked me go into municipal court, stand in the back, and when a certain case was called simply say, "I'd like a continuance, Your Honor." I refused on the grounds that I would be practicing law without a license. The lawyer shook his head and walked away. That was the dim view that those three brothers took of the law.

After working for them it's no wonder that I left law school after a year and a half without graduating. I hate the phrase "flunked out." I failed to complete the assigned courses. I have my explanation for what happened, and the school has theirs.

Let's get the school's out of the way first. There was some sort of important test that had to be taken for me to advance, but I missed it. My explanation was that I was going to law school in the morning, working as a law clerk in the afternoon, and then at night I was performing with the Oak Park Players, a local theater group. Something had to give, and it was law school.

Law school did give me an appreciation for the precise word. Lawyers have to nail every phrase, or constantly be in danger of an adversary exposing a loophole. Nevertheless, I have noticed that they often throw many similar-meaning words together just to cover the gray area. To wit: "I hereby assign, convey, bequeath, and transfer now, forever, and in perpetuity . . ."

Had I taken that test and stuck out law school, I always figured that I would have pursued trial law because trial lawyers are actors. They stand in front of judges and juries and entertain them with borderline preposterous stories—not unlike those told by stand-ups, come to think of it.

Despite my law school experience, I seldom tell lawyer jokes. They're too easy and too clichéd. Ah, what the heck. What's the difference between a snake and a lawyer? If there's an accident, there are no skid marks in front of the lawyer.

•

In 1952, I was drafted. At the time I entered the army, the Korean War was going on. When I reported to Fort Sheridan in Illinois, I met with the admitting officer about my posting. He informed me that I was going to be assigned to the infantry, probably as field wireman. Now, field wireman is the worst job you could receive. The field wireman is the guy who climbs the telephone poles on the battlefield and reconnects the power. The North Koreans sharpened their aim by taking out the field wiremen.

The admitting officer asked me if I had a degree. I told him that I did, in management. He then asked me whether it was in factory or personnel management. Thinking quickly and reasoning that the military didn't have many factories—and therefore little use for factory managers—I told him it was in personnel management.

"You're very lucky because it takes a direct order from the Secretary of the Army to send you overseas to Korea," he explained. "You have what's called an M.O.S., a military occupational specialty designation 1290."

So instead of becoming a field wireman in training, I reported to basic training at Camp Roberts in California as a 1290. I went about acquainting myself with A.R.s (army regulations) and S.R.s (special regulations). While reading the A.R.s, to become proficient as a personnel management specialist, I came across the actual text of the order that dictated 1290s could only be sent overseas by a direct order from the Secretary of the Army.

Unfortunately, I found a small hitch. The regulation had been instated in 1946 because personnel managers were needed at home to help expedite soldiers leaving the service and ensure their files were in order. However, the regulation was rescinded in 1948, four years before I was drafted. My admitting officer apparently didn't know this, and I sure wasn't about to say anything.

Every month, the P.O.R. list—processing for reassignment—was posted, listing the guys who would be shipping out for Korea. Everyone would get up early on those days to check the list for shipping orders or relief. I never bothered to go down to check because I knew my name wouldn't be on it.

I was also given an IQ test. The combination of my score and my college degree in personnel management made me eligible for officer school. I told them, no thanks. I was stuck in the service for two years, and I didn't see any reason to stay another year just to become a second lieutenant.

After basic training, I was transferred to San Francisco and assigned to a personnel management team. Our group traveled up and down the West Coast auditing personnel records at military bases. The truth is that we were most concerned about making the system work for our comfort and entertainment.

In exciting places like Tacoma and Los Angeles, we always found trouble with the records. We'd be scheduled for three days, but upon arrival, we would send word to our warrant officer that things were a mess and we'd need at least a week to straighten them out. However, at Camp Irwin in the hot, desolate California desert, everything was always spotless, and we were out of there in a day.

When our team arrived at a new base, we explained to the officer in charge that we were carrying top secret material and therefore needed a lock on our door. So instead of sleeping in the barracks on cots, we were each given our own room in the non-commissioned officers' quarters.

Before inspection each morning, we'd padlock our door and leave just enough space so they could inspect the room—but not enough to see that only the area visible through the crack was made up. Sure, it would have taken another four minutes to clean up the rest of the room, but that was beside the point. We did it to buck the system.

•

During the two years I was in the service, I saw the inefficiencies and the waste—to which I admittedly made my own very small contribution. This experience formed the basis of one of my first routines, "The Cruise of the U.S.S. *Codfish*" ("The Submarine Commander" for short). It was all about how someone totally unqualified can rise three levels above their competency because the organization is so big that the right hand doesn't know what the left hand is doing. Though I was in the army, I set the routine in the navy. Somehow, a submarine commander was funnier than a platoon leader.

After a two-year journey, the U.S.S. *Codfish* submarine is about to surface, and the submarine commander addresses his men:

I know you are all anxious to be reunited with your loved ones—in some cases your wives—but we have a few moments before we surface and I've just jotted down some things I think are important. I wouldn't take the time if I didn't think so. First of all, I think we ought to give the cooks a standing ovation for the wonderful jobs they've done. So if you men want to stand right now.... Let's really hear it for the cooks. I don't think you men realize what a difficult problem it is.... Come on, let's let bygones be bygones and hear it for the cooks.... Men, I'm not going to surface until we hear it for the cooks.... All right, that's better.

Today, as we add another glorious page to the story of the

U.S.S. Codfish, *I think it's important that we reflect on some of the past glories of the U.S.S.* Codfish. *I don't know if you men know this, but the* Codfish *holds the record for the most Japanese tonnage sunk, being comprised of five freighters and fifteen aircraft carriers—a truly enviable record. Unfortunately, they were sunk in 1954. However, it stands as the largest peacetime tonnage ever sunk.*

Our voyage has received a lot of coverage in the newspapers, and I would like to present our side of it.... I think our firing on Miami Beach can best be termed "ill-timed." It happened on what they call in the newspaper business a "slow news day," and as a result, received a lot more space than I think it deserved, especially since it was the off-season down there.

Men, I think you'll agree I've been pretty lax as far as discipline is concerned, and, golly, nobody enjoys a joke more than me, but I'd like the executive officer returned.... Now, we've looked in the torpedo tubes, we've looked in your bags.... It's been more than two weeks, men. We're just damn lucky it wasn't the navigational officer or someone real important like that....

Looking back on the mutiny, I think a lot of the trouble stemmed from the fact that you men weren't coming to me with your problems. As I told you, the door to my office is always open.... I think you know why it's always open. It was stolen. I'd like that returned. It looks like the work of the same man.

Since we started the cruise on such a low note, I think it's important that we end it on a high note. To me, there is nothing more impressive in the navy than when a submarine breaks water to see a bunch of sailors in their dress blues as

they come rushing up out of the, the, the … that hole there …
and come to parade rest. … Oh, all right. I've just been noti-
fied that we will be surfacing in a moment, and you'll be
happy to know that you will be gazing on the familiar sky-
line of either New York City or Buenos Aires. Dismissed,
men. That's all.

•

My first real jobs in the workforce were back in Chicago
in accounting. From 1956 to 1957, I worked as an accountant in the engineering department at U.S. Gypsum,
a company that manufactured wallboard and drywall.
They offered me a full-time position and asked me to re-
locate to Poland Spring, Maine. Had I moved there and
lost my job at U.S. Gypsum, who knows, I might have
ended up getting in on the ground floor of the bottled water business. But I couldn't see myself living in Maine, at
least not in Poland Spring.

After refusing the transfer, and leaving U.S. Gypsum, I
accepted a job in the accounting department for the Glidden Company in downtown Chicago. As your basic nine-to-
five bookkeeper, I had several responsibilities, including
reconciling the records between the company's different
divisions.

Another of my daily tasks was monitoring petty cash. It
was in this area that I developed and implemented my odd
theory of accounting: If you got within a couple of bucks,
it was okay. Although my theory never caught on, it really
does work.

Each time a salesman would come in off the road and

turn in a receipt for ten dollars for gas, I would give him the cash and put the receipt in the petty-cash drawer. Another guy might come in with a credit card receipt for thirty bucks for a hotel room and a meal, and I'd count out three ten-dollar bills and file the credit card receipt.

At the end of each day, I had to reconcile what was in the cash drawer with the receipts. It was always close, but it never balanced. At five o'clock sharp, everybody in the accounting department would leave the office. I would be the only one left, tearing my hair out over why petty cash was short by $1.48. Usually around eight o'clock, I'd find the discrepancy.

I followed this routine for a couple of weeks until I grew completely frustrated. Finally one day, as everybody was leaving at five and I was facing a couple more hours of work, I pulled the $1.67 that I was short out of my pocket, put it in the cash drawer, and called it a day.

A few days later, the petty cash drawer was over by $2.11, so I took $2.11 out of petty cash and pocketed it. I was hardly stealing. Inevitably, in the next couple of days I would be under, and back the money would go.

After several weeks, Mr. Hutchinson, who was head of the accounting department for the Glidden Company, discovered my shortcut to balancing petty cash.

"George," he lectured me. "These are not sound accounting principles."

Back then, I went by George, from my given name George Robert Newhart. When I was growing up, most people called me George. However, because my father's name was also George, I was called Bob around the house, and my close friends picked up on this. But I wasn't a junior; my dad was George David Newhart, and his father was George Michael Newhart. So all through high school and college, I was George. In the army, I was George. Basically, on any form that required block capital letters, I was GEORGE.

"You know, Mr. Hutchinson, I don't think I'm cut out for accounting, because this makes absolutely perfect sense to me," I explained. "Why would you pay me six dollars an hour to spend three or four hours finding a dollar-forty? It's much easier if I just make up the difference out of my own pocket because I'll get it back next week."

•

To pass the time during the tedious afternoons of balancing petty cash, I began swapping absurd stories on the telephone with my friend Ed Gallagher, who worked in advertising. I'd call Ed and identify myself as, say, the plant manger of a yeast factory:

"Sir, it's Mr. Tompkins and we have a problem at your yeast factory. There's a fire. . . . Hold on, sir. I have to put you on hold while I run up another floor. The yeast is rising. . . . Sir, are you still there? The firefighters are on-site trying to contain the blaze. . . . Hold on, sir. I have to run up another flight of stairs. . . ."

The next time I'd be an airline pilot:

"Mr. Gallagher, you don't know me but I'm a United Airlines pilot. I just picked your name out of the telephone book. We took off from Midway Airport a half hour ago, but the copilot and I got to horsing around in the cabin, and we both fell out. The plane is still up there with fifty-seven people onboard. I tried to call Midway and tell them about it, but they said 'Why don't you leave us alone?' and hung up on me. I thought you might call and explain things."

A friend of ours named Chris Petersen heard about the routines and offered to put up the money for us to record them and send them to radio stations, in exchange for a share of the profits. Ed and I decided to give it a try. It beat working a "day" job.

Ed and I recorded routines that were extensions of our phone conversations. With Chris's financial support, we mailed out one hundred demo tapes to radio stations around the country.

Three radio stations wrote back and asked how much we wanted for the routines. They were located in Jacksonville, Florida; Idaho Falls, Idaho; and Northampton, Massachusetts. Picking a number out of the air, we decided to charge $7.50 per week for five minutes of sketches. This seemed like a good deal for us. All we had to pay for were the acetate tapes and postage. We used the recording studio at the Leo Burnett offices where Ed worked. On recording days, we waited until the offices emptied out in the evening and worked clandestinely into the night.

Not long after we made our deal with the three stations, Ed contracted pneumonia and we didn't record for two weeks. By the time he recovered, we had one night to record ten routines and have the packages postmarked by midnight. Otherwise we would be in violation of our contract.

To prepare, I had sketched out a few notes, but they were hardly radio-ready scripts. Ed and I met at the Leo Burnett offices in the early evening. Basically, Ed asked me what I wanted to be, and I said, "a card-section coach being interviewed on 'Your Sports Corner.' "

Then we'd improvise:

Ed: "I guess most football fans are familiar with the card section. These are made up of students who hold cards and manipulate them to form designs. You've probably seen them at football games all over the country. Tonight we have with us the coach of the Midland College card section. His name, of course, is Denut Crown. He's one of the best card-section coaches in the country. Coach Crown, it's good to have you on the show."

Coach: "Hi, Ed. It's nice to be on your show."

Ed: "At Midland, probably your most famous portrait, your famous maneuver with your card section is this portrait of Lincoln that you do."

Coach: "That seems to go over the best."

Ed: "You consider that your greatest?"

Coach: "Yes, I would say, at least from the fans' viewpoint. They seem to enjoy that the most."

Ed: "How do you look this coming year?"

Coach: "Well, Ed, we're kind of in the dog days in Midland. We've had, as you know, five national champions. This year, we've lost both of Lincoln's eyebrows to graduation, and in February, we are going to lose his left ear."

Ed: "Gee, that's a shame. That's probably going to raise havoc with your team."

Coach: "It really is, but we think that within two or three years we're gonna have another fine card-section team."

Ed: "Speaking of a fine card-section team and about all-

American mention time . . . who would you say are the greats of your former card section?"

Coach: "Ah, gee, Ed, I don't know. We've had so many good boys. Of course, whenever you think of card sections, you think of names like Up-Fingers Doolan, Lightnin' Larry Strickland, Terrible Tommy Wolf, and, of course, the greatest lefty of them all, Lefty Lawrence."

Ed: "Lefty Lawrence? . . . Well, if I had to name an all-American card section, I think I would want all of those boys on my team and, most especially, Lefty Lawrence. Now, tell me, what made Lefty great?"

Coach: "Well, Ed, maybe I can give you an example of just what Lefty's greatness consisted of. It was in 1947. We had a wonderful card section. . . ."

Ed: "I remember that one . . ."

Coach: "It wasn't as good as '28, I don't think . . ."

Ed: "Well, you won the award in '47 and '28."

Coach: "We did, but I think the '28 team was pretty good."

Ed: "Anyway, Lefty Lawrence was part of that '47 team."

Coach: "We had a little problem. Of course, Lefty . . . his best position was in the eyebrows. Everyone knew that. He was probably the best. . . ."

Ed: "He was pretty much an eyebrow man. . . ."

Coach: "He was one of the best eyebrow men in the game for all time, I would say. I had to take him out of the eyebrow and throw him into the beard because we had a depth problem there. We needed a man—"

Ed: "In the beard? How did he take that switch?"

Coach: "He adjusted right away. That's the amazing thing. And then later in the year, just to prove his greatness even further, I had to shove him into Lincoln's nose and he had no problem at all adjusting there. I think that's the sign of a truly great card-section man."

Ed: "Well, I think you are being overly modest there. I think we can attribute most of the credit to you. Coach Denut Crown of Midland College."

Next, Ed and I rooted through the agency's sound-effects records used for television commercials. We found a nice recording of a train crash. Using the train crash as the blow-off, or sound effect, we worked backward and wrote a routine. The entire story led up to this climactic sound effect, such as Ed playing his typical straight-man interviewer and me as Gasper Hollingsferry, the head train-switcher and dispatcher at the Central Shipping Yard.

It went a little bit like this:

Ed: "Say, I've noticed that there's a tremendous amount of buttons and panels, and, of course, as I look out here through these windows and into the yard, I see these miles and miles of track crisscrossing each other, how do you keep track of all of them, Mr. Hollingsferry?"

Bob: "Well, it's mostly about trial and error. It took me about four weeks to learn. After the first week, you find you make quite a few mistakes. Then the second week it's less, and the third week it's less, and by the end of the fourth week, you got the yards down pretty well."

Ed: "It seems to me an awfully dangerous way to go about teaching a switchman his business. You don't have any supervisors? You don't have any textbooks?"

Bob: "Well, we tried textbooks. We used both methods.

It's sort of expensive, but when you see the cars strewn all over the yard like that, it makes quite an impression and you very seldom will switch them onto that track again. We find it's the best method."

Ed: "That certainly is interesting."

Bob: (Aside to Ed's crew) "Uh, I thought I told you guys you're gonna have to keep your wires and cords off the tracks. We've got trains coming through here daily——"

Ed: "Well, speaking of trains, sir, I'm sorry to interrupt, but down here on the main track it looks to me as if those two trains are going to crash."

Bob: "Yeah. . . . Those two'll crash."

Ed: "You say those two are going to crash. Aren't you going to do anything about it?"

Bob: "No, I never got a D-07 on those trains."

Ed: "A D-07, sir?"

Bob: "That's a form we have whenever they find a mistake and we switch a train onto the wrong track, as these two obviously are. We're supposed to get a D-07. I can't touch these levers until I get a D-07."

Ed: "Well, sir, you mean to say that you'll sit here without using the handbrake to stop these two trains from crashing?"

Bob: "It's not my fault. It's somebody in the main office."

Ed: "I fully realize that, sir. . . . So you mean to say you are going to sit here and do absolutely nothing?"

Bob: "If we were to do away with a D-07, as you're obviously suggesting, we'd have nothing but plain chaos. . . ."

(A loud *crash* is heard.)

Ed: "Well, thank you very much, Mr. Hollingsferry. We now take you back to your announcer."

And the routine fades out to the sound of flames crackling and chaos.

With that, I dashed to the post office with the tapes.

Soon we discovered that we hadn't costed things out very well. Worse still, we didn't immediately realize this because we didn't bill until after thirteen weeks.

On paper, we were earning $22.50 a week from three radio stations, but we were spending forty. That left us with a loss of nearly $18 a week. Then one of the radio stations refused to pay, so it turned out we were only collecting $15 a week, leaving us $25 a week in the red. After thirteen weeks, we had lost $325 on the venture, and our comedy enterprise collapsed in financial ruin.

When the other two stations asked to renew our contracts, we wrote back and told them that we couldn't afford it. You don't have to be an accountant to figure that out.

CHAPTER FOUR

Part-time Jobs
That Sustained Me

Still, I didn't intend to be a stand-up comedian. I just wanted to see if I could somehow make a living at being funny. I had to find out if what people had been telling me up to that point in my life was true—that I was funny. I had to leave the world of accounting and see if I could earn a living at being funny. That was the drive. I had to find out. I couldn't live my entire life not knowing. Even if I flopped, at least I would have known that I tried comedy, I couldn't make a living at it, and I was only funny to my friends.

My partnership with Ed had been on hold ever since we figured out how much money we were losing. It officially ended when he was offered a position at the BBDO ad agency in New York. Ed had a wife and two sons to support, so he accepted the job. His feeling was that we had fun, we didn't make any money, and it was something that we could always be proud of doing. But the bottom line was that he had to provide for his family.

Unlike Ed, I had no obligation to anybody except myself. I was single and living at home, so I decided to take part-time jobs to tide me over financially until I was able to somehow make a living at being funny. I admit it wasn't a foolproof career plan, and it was one I often questioned.

I always liked the Christmas season because part-time jobs were plentiful. Stores like Goldblatts and V, L & A, a subsidiary of Abercrombie & Fitch, were always hiring part-timers.

One year when I was working at V, L & A in the cigar, cigarette, and pipe department, a salesman from the camera department asked if I would watch his station so he could go to lunch. A customer came in and began looking around. I knew nothing about cameras, but I asked the gentleman if he needed help.

"There is one thing," the man said in a Connecticut malocclusion. "I cannot find good batteries. I travel to Africa and the humidity saps the energy from my camera batteries. For the life of me, I haven't been able to find batteries that last a fortnight in Africa."

I thought to myself, well, I think I've got problems. I'm moping around because I don't have a regular job, the radio show isn't working, my friends are getting married, buying houses, and starting families, and I'm not going anywhere in life. I need to stop feeling sorry for myself and put myself in this guy's shoes. This poor bastard can't find batteries that work in Africa.

My biggest and most harrowing sale at V, L & A happened one afternoon when a very dapper gentleman came into the store and placed a large order for crystal plunger ashtrays shaped like roulette wheels with accompanying lighters. I rang up his purchase, and the bill came to $3,000.

I asked the customer, whom I didn't immediately recognize, if he would like these gift-wrapped and sent, and he said that he would.

"Could you give me your name, please?"

"It's Anthony."

"And your last name, please?"

"It's Accardo. Anthony Accardo."

If life all comes down to a few moments, then this was one of them. Anyone who grew up in Chicago, particularly on the West Side, was familiar with this name: Anthony "Big Tuna" Accardo was, for forty years, the reputed head of the Chicago mob, which was affectionately known as "the outfit." Accardo had gotten his start as a bodyguard and "special enforcer" to Al Capone. There was no way I could screw this order up.

I carefully wrote down Mr. Accardo's address in River Forest, a tony suburb. Then I felt it was incumbent upon me for his full customer satisfaction, as well as for my own personal safety, to explain to him the ordering and shipping process.

"Mr. Accardo," I said, "I'm going to take your presents, and I am going to put them over there." I pointed across the room to a table piled high with gift boxes. "The shipping department will pick them up from over there." Again I pointed across the room, away from my workstation. "So if any of them should arrive damaged in any way, that would be the responsibility of the shipping department. Being over here in sales, I would have nothing to do with that."

•

The reason I accepted only part-time jobs was because I didn't want to give the impression to a company that I had any intention of staying on. I felt it was only fair to inform them that I would be there only on a temporary basis and they, in turn, would acknowledge that they only needed me for a short time. This eliminated any of the B.S. of the guy who professes his long-term loyalty to the company, but really just wants to make as much money as he can in three months so he can buy a convertible and move to California.

Stating my intention didn't stop the occasional full-time offer from coming my way. When I worked at the Illinois State Compensation Board, they tried to extend me. It was a six-week job, and they had advertised it as a six-week job. Looking back, there were several possibilities why they wanted to keep me on.

One guy I trained would have been better off on the other side of the counter. He was a musician who usually had a hangover from whatever booze or drug he had consumed the night before. As his supervisor, I instructed him on how to file the unemployment claims, a tedious process by which each claim was catalogued by the last four digits of the claimant's Social Security number.

This fella wasn't the brightest guy. One day he had a headache at lunch, so he decided to take an Alka-Seltzer. In those days, each Alka-Seltzer tablet had a plastic protective coating around it. So I sat there watching him drop the plastic-covered Alka-Seltzer into a cup, waiting for it to dissolve, and then repeating the process. Nobody else seemed to notice him, but I was fascinated watching him futilely push this tablet to the bottom and then curse in frustration at its refusal to dissolve. It was one of those oddities that stuck with me.

After he had been working for me for about a month, I hired a young woman. I was training her, explaining that we filed the claims by the last four digits of the claimant's Social Security number. I handed her some files and told her to get started.

The hungover musician walked over to me and asked what I had just said to the new employee.

"I told her how to file, by the last four numbers of the people's Social Security numbers," I said.

He furrowed his brow. "I thought you said to file these by the *first* four numbers."

I shook my head at the realization that every one of his claims needed to be refiled.

Man, I'd love to know what he's doing now.

But the real reason the Illinois State Compensation Board wanted to keep me on was because most people who had held my job quickly figured out the game. I worked five days a week and earned sixty dollars, while the unemployed were collecting fifty-five—and they only had to come in one day a week. I admit it took six weeks, but it finally dawned on me that I was coming in four extra days a week for a measly five extra bucks.

•

A potential career break came when Dan Sorkin called me one day and asked me what I was doing on Saturday. Dan was a popular Chicago disk jockey who liked my routines, and I had appeared on his radio show several times. Like Jean Shepherd in New York and Don Sherwood in San Francisco, Dan was the voice of Chicago, so when he called you listened.

Dan told me to meet him at Meigs Field, a small downtown airport on Lake Michigan that is no longer there. A radio station in Grand Rapids, Michigan, was looking for a new disk jockey. We were going to fly there in his single-engine Bonanza plane and get me that job.

To bolster my credentials, Dan had told the Grand Rapids station that I was living in Texas but wanted to move back to Chicago. If the station wanted to hire me, it was going to cost them a lot of money because I really wanted to be in Chicago.

We boarded Dan's single-engine Bonanza, and he asked if I wanted to fly across the lake or along the shoreline, down around Gary, Indiana. No-brainer: the shoreline.

When we arrived in Grand Rapids, the station managers began chatting up Dan, the legendary voice of Chicago. They gave Bob Newhart, who incidentally had no experience in radio broadcasting, a commercial to read and sent me to a sound booth.

Thankfully, they were all so interested in what Dan had to say that they didn't pay any attention to me. I started to read the commercial copy, but I was so nervous that I kept mispronouncing the words. I waved from inside the booth to get their attention so I could do a retake—all to no avail. Dan was regaling them with stories.

After a bout of nervous laughter, I finally finished the copy. Emerging from the booth, I told Dan that we had better be getting back to Chicago. I didn't want them to hear my laughingly laughable demo tape.

On the return trip, 2,200 feet over the steel plant smokestacks of Gary, Indiana, Dan turned around and informed me, "The engine is going to cut out, but don't let that bother you."

I quickly forgot about the botched audition. "What?"

"The engine is going to stop because I have to switch fuel tanks," he said, adding reassuringly, "but it will start up again."

Sure enough, the propeller stopped spinning. We glided for a few minutes and, thank god, it soon whirred back to life. I closed my eyes for the rest of the flight.

As we prepared to land at Meigs Field, Dan yelled out, "Look at that view of the skyline! Isn't it incredible?" I kept my eyes sealed shut. I didn't care if I ever saw another airplane in my life.

Needless to say, we never heard from Grand Rapids.

•

I wrote most of my material in a vacuum, having no idea when, where, or if the routines would ever be performed. My best routines had a catalyst that I often discovered by chance. The idea for my routine "Abe Lincoln vs. Madison Avenue" originated from a book titled *The Hidden Persuaders*, which talked about the danger of PR men creating images in presidential campaigns to the degree that you were voting for a personality rather than a leader's ideology.

In the piece, I imagined a telephone conversation between the press agent and Abraham Lincoln just before Gettysburg, that I think, in part, would have gone something like this:

Hi Abe, sweetheart. How are you, kid? How's Gettysburg?... Sort of a drag, heh? Well, Abe you know them small Pennsylvania towns, you seen one you seen 'em all.... Listen Abe, I got the note. What's the problem?.... You're thinking of shaving it off? Abe, don't you see that's part of the image with the shawl and the stovepipe hat and the string tie?... You don't have the shawl. Where's the shawl?.... You left it in Washington. What are you wearing, Abe?...A sort of cardigan? Abe, don't you see that doesn't fit with the string tie and the beard? Abe, would you leave the beard on and get the shawl?

Now, what's this about Grant?... You're getting a lot of complaints about Grant's drinking. Abe, to be perfectly honest with you, I don't see the problem. You knew he was a lush when you appointed him.... Your gag writers... You want to come back with something funny? Maybe an anecdote about a town drunk. I can't promise anything. I'll get them working on it.

Abe, you got the speech....Abe, you haven't changed the speech, have you?... Oh, Abe. What do ya change the speeches for?...A couple of minor changes?...I'll bet. All right, what are they?... You what? You typed it! Abe, how many times have we told you—on the backs of envelopes.... I understand it's harder to read that way, but it looks like you wrote it on the train coming down. Abe, could you do this: Could you memorize it and then put it on the back of an envelope? We are getting a lot of play in the press on that. How are the envelopes holding out?...You could stand another box.

What else, Abe?...You changed "four score and seven" to "eighty-seven"?...I understand it means the same thing, Abe. That's meant to be a grabber....Abe, we test-marketed that in Erie and they went out of their minds.... Well, Abe, it's sort of like Marc Antony saying, "Friends, Romans, countrymen, I've got something I want to tell you." You see what I mean, Abe?...What else?..."People will little note nor long remember"...Abe, what could possibly be wrong with that?...They'll remember it. It's the old humble bit. You can't say, "It's a great speech, I think everybody is going to remember it." You'll come off as a braggart, don't you see that?...Abe, do the speech the way Charlie wrote it, would ya? The inaugural swung, didn't it?

Abe, hold on. They've come up with a thing on Grant.... Good, ah beautiful! They got a beautiful squelch on Grant. You tell them you are going to find out what brand he drinks and then send bottles to all his generals.

Saturday night...I'm going to be in New York Saturday night....A bridge party at the White House...Listen, Abe, why don't you take in a play?

When I wrote the routine, I was living at home. I gave the routine to my mother to read.

"Do men really call each other 'sweetheart'?" she asked me.

"Yes, Mom, in advertising they do."

I performed the routine on Dan Sorkin's show, which

led to a phone call from the producer of the local Emmy Awards, not the national one. He was looking for performers for the show, which would be held in the lobby of the Tribune Building. It turned out that IATSE, the film technicans' union, was on strike, so they couldn't televise the show. He asked me if I would perform, and I gladly accepted.

After I did "Abe Lincoln," a local anchorman named Alex Dryer took the stage and declared, "What do you mean there's no talent in Chicago?"

As a result of the high praise for my appearance at the non-televised, local Emmy Awards, I was hired in 1958 to appear on a man-in-the-street program on WBKB, the ABC affiliate in Chicago. The show was hosted by Tom Mercein, a local announcer. Tom's son Chuck later played for the Giants, which is neither here nor there, but I thought I would mention it.

My role on the show was to supply the comic relief. Tom was the roving reporter who would walk up to me and interview me. I played a different person every day, and many of the characters were drawn from my unsold radio routines.

One day I was Dr. Arnold Currothers, a physician and surgeon. Tom buttonholed Dr. Currothers, who discussed his surgery of the previous evening.

"I got a call about ten-thirty P.M. from one of my patients for an emergency appendectomy," Dr. Currothers told him. "I got down to the hospital around eleven o'clock, and we had the patient on the operating table around eleven-thirty. And then I opened the patient up around twelve o'clock. Then we ran into complications with the operation . . . and I closed the patient up at, uh, I closed the, uh, I'm sure I closed the patient up . . ."

With that, the good doctor took off running back to the hospital.

I had to be at the studio at 7:30 A.M., and the show aired from 8:30 to 9:00, opposite the *Today* show and *Captain Kangaroo*. Given the competition and lack of viewer response, we weren't sure the signal was even getting out of the building. Still, I felt like I had died and gone to heaven. I was making $300 a week, and I was finished working at 10 A.M. I'd catch the bus home, grab my golf clubs, and be on the first tee by noon. I couldn't imagine life would ever get any better than that.

Occasionally I would stay a few extra hours to be an in-studio guest. For these segments, I would write the questions for Tom and he would interview me, in character.

Once I was a baseball player, and not a very good one. I held the record for having lived in the most cities in one year because I was constantly being traded.

"What's the longest you've lived in one city?" Tom asked.

"Two weeks," I replied. "It was really great. We put the kids in the school and led a normal life."

The show aired for sixteen weeks, during which time we received a grand total of one piece of mail. Actually, it was a postcard, referring to an old routine that Ed Gallagher and I had done where a talk-show host interviews me as Patrick M. Doyle, noted lecturer and author of nineteen books.

Host: "That's a tremendous output. It just shows your versatility and your tremendous profundity, wouldn't you say?"

Doyle: "Well, no, I wouldn't say it, but I'd like for you to say it."

Host: "Tell me, Pat. Are all these books in English? What I mean by that is, are there any foreign printings?"

Doyle: "Well, just one book. It's printed in English and French."

Host: "Really. What's the name of that?"

Doyle: "It was an English-French dictionary."

Later in the interview, the host asks me to pick a favorite book from the nineteen, all of which, he points out, have a human-interest element, give a tug at the heartstrings, and have happy endings so you are glad that you read them.

I tell the host that one of my favorites was about Court, a cocker spaniel who was owned by the Addams family in Scranton, Pennsylvania. The family was very protective of the dog, and they never let him outside because he was so small. But he happened to find a board loose in the fence one day, and he crawled out into the alley. The mother was panicked when she couldn't find the dog. Then the kids came home, and they were hysterical that their puppy was missing.

As Patrick M. Doyle tells the story, he becomes so overcome with emotion at the thought of the lost dog that he breaks down crying. He's wailing so uncontrollably that his speech turns into gibberish. As the show fades out, the host pleads that the time is growing short and begs Doyle to tell him if they ever found the dog.

In the postcard—the sole piece of mail received by *The Tom Mercein Show*—a viewer wondered where he could buy the Patrick M. Doyle book with the story of Court in it so he could find out what happened to the dog.

•

These were lean years financially, but I avoided starvation by living in my parents' house until I was twenty-nine. One year, I asked a friend named John Kelly if someone at his accounting firm could figure my income tax. John gave my paperwork to a colleague at the firm. That year I had earned all of $1,100.

His colleague took one look and said to John, "Does this guy have a paper route?"

"No," John said, "I went to college with him."

The fact of the matter was that my friends were married, buying houses and cars, preparing to start families, and I wasn't really doing anything. There was a point at which I thought, "You have really majorly screwed up. Look at what you have done to your life."

My parents had no idea what I was doing, but I did. I was trying to find a way to break into the comedy business. Until that happened, each morning I would pore over the want ads in the *Chicago Tribune*, looking for yet another part-time job.

One typical morning, I came across a full-page ad for driving instructors. It occurred to me that I had seen this ad the day before and the day before that. The ad was what is called a "standing ad," meaning that it runs every day. Presumably, that meant there was a continuous need for that position due to constant turnover.

I began to wonder why there was an insatiable need for driving instructors. This led me to imagine what an average day was like for driving instructors. Then I exaggerated it a little bit and what I arrived at was: a group of men who go to work every day and never know for sure if they'll return home that night because they face death in a hundred different ways.

I sat down and wrote a routine, despite the fact that I had no place to sell it or perform it. I now give you "The Driving Instructor" in its entirety for what I think is a pretty good payoff:

How do you do, Mrs. Webb. I see you have had one lesson already. Who was the instructor on that, Mrs. Webb? . . . Mr. Adams. . . . I'm sorry. Here it is. . . . Just let me read ahead here and kind of familiarize myself with the case. . . . How fast were you going when Mr. Adams jumped from the car? . . . Seventy-five. And where was that? . . . In your driveway. How far had Mr. Adams gotten in the lesson? . . . Backing out. I see. You were backing out at seventy-five and that's when he jumped.

Did he cover starting the car? . . . . And the other way of stopping? What's the other way of stopping? . . . Throwing it in reverse. That would do it, you're right. All right, you want to start the car. Mrs. Webb, you just turned on the lights. You want to start the car. . . . They all look alike, don't they? I don't know why they designed them that way.

Let's pull out into traffic. What's the first thing we are going to do? What did Mr. Adams tell you to do before he let you pull out in traffic? . . . . Besides praying. No, what I had in mind was checking the rearview mirror. You see, we always want to check the rearview. . . . DON'T PULL OUT! Please don't cry. I'm sorry, but there was this bus, Mrs. Webb. All right, the lane is clear now, you want to pull out. That wasn't bad at all. You might try it a little slower next time. All right, let's get up a bit more speed and gradually ease it into second. . . . Well, I didn't want to cover reverse this early, but as long as you shifted into it. . . . Of course, you're nervous. I'm nervous. I'm not just saying that, I'm really very nervous. Just don't pay any attention to their honking. You're doing fine. . . . You're not blocking anyone's lane. . . . No, as long as you are here on the safety island, you are not blocking anyone's lane.

All right, you want to start the car. While you're turning the lights off, why don't you turn off the heater? There we are. Let's get up a bit of speed. Now let's practice some turns. The important thing on turns is not to make them too sharp, just kind of make a gradual . . . Now that was fine. That was a wonderful turn. It's hard for me to believe you've only had one lesson after you make a turn like that. Are you sure you haven't had more than that? One little thing—this is a one-way street. . . . No, actually, it's partly my fault. You were in the left-hand lane and you were signaling left, and I just more or less assumed you were going to turn left. . . . Same to you, fella! . . . I don't know what he said, Mrs. Webb. Let's pull into the alley up there and practice a little alley driving. This is something a lot of the schools leave out and we think is— You're going too fast, Mrs. Webb! You were up around sixty and it's kind of a sharp turn.

Just drive down the alley there, Mrs. Webb. Maybe we'd better stop here. I don't think you are going to make it between the truck and the building. . . . Mrs. Webb . . . Mrs. Webb! . . . Mrs. Webb! . . . I really didn't think you were going to make it. That just shows you we can be wrong, too.... No, I'll get out on your side, that's all right. Mrs. Webb, it might be a good idea if we went over to the driving area. They have a student driver area a few blocks away. Maybe traffic throws you, maybe that's the problem. We'll turn here and it's only about a block up. Turn right, here.... That was my fault again. You see, I meant the next street, not this man's lawn.... Sir, sir, would you mind turning off the sprinkler for a moment.... Newly seeded, is that right? That's always the way, isn't it.... I don't suppose it is so damn funny, is it?...

Mrs. Webb, do you want to back out and get off?... Creeping bend, that's right.... Just back out, Mrs. Webb.... Thank you very much, sir.... Ah, now we hit someone. Remember, you were going to watch the rearview mirror, remember we covered that?... The red light blinded you.... The flashing red light blinded you... the flashing red light on the car you hit blinded you?... Yes, Officer, she was just telling me about it. All right, all right. Mrs. Webb, I am going to have to go with the officer to the police station.... They don't believe it and they'd like me to describe it. Now, the other officer is going to drive you back to the driving school, and then you are to meet us at the police station....

My name is Frank Dexter, Mrs. Webb. Why do you ask?... You want to be sure and get me *next time!*

Now, I hope you agree that's pretty detailed with regard to driving. They are drilling the basics: checking the rearview mirror, avoiding one-way streets, and maneuvering through a narrow alley. All this is pretty run-of-the-mill for most of you, because you have probably been driving for a number of years.

Strange but true: At the time I wrote "The Driving In-structor," I didn't have a driver's license. The reason I didn't have a driver's license was simple: I didn't know how to drive.

Most of the guys I grew up with were taught how to drive by their fathers. My dad just never got around to teaching me. He had a car, albeit one with sand in the gas tank, but he never showed me how to drive it.

Even as a young adult, I didn't bother to learn. I took the L or the bus to and from everywhere I needed to go in Chicago. In any event, I couldn't afford to buy a car, so what was the point of learning to drive? Where would I go?

> > > > > >

CHAPTER FIVE

The Funniest Guy on the Corner

On February 10, 1960, I was admitted to a very exclusive club—the fraternity of stand-up comics. It isn't the most exclusive club in the United States. The most exclusive club is former presidents. Currently, there are just four alive: Gerald Ford, Jimmy Carter, Bill Clinton, and George H. W. Bush. The next most exclusive club would be owners of NFL teams, of which there are thirty. But then right after that would be working stand-up comedians, and I became one that February evening.

But I'm getting a little bit ahead of myself.

I had never intended to perform my material as a stand-up in front of an audience with a telephone as my partner. A comedian named Don Adams changed my mind about that.

It was very early on in my career, and the line of work I was in—comedy—wasn't making me any money. No regular employment had resulted from the radio tapes that Ed and I made or the brief guest spot on the man-on-the-street TV show, and I was still working part-time day jobs waiting for something to break. I decided to become a comedy writer and sell my material to established comedians.

I felt "The Submarine Commander" could very easily be adapted to Don Adams because of his deadpan delivery. The routine involves a commander of a nuclear submarine whose troops run roughshod over him on his final voyage. I reached Don when he was in Chicago for a show and he agreed to take a look.

I later learned that Don did the routine for his wife, Dorothy. When she told him she thought it was funny, Don replied in that William Powell–esque clipped voice of his: "It's not! And I'm not paying for it!"

He didn't pay for it, but he used it. He told me that it wasn't the type of material he was looking for. He gave me his address in New York and told me to send along anything else I wrote that might be right for him. Two weeks later, I was watching *The Steve Allen Show*, and Don walked out onstage and performed a chunk of "The Submarine Commander." Word for word. I couldn't believe it. I was yelling at the TV, "That's mine! You're stealing my routine!"

I was furious. To put it mildly, I felt that Don was not a very stand-up stand-up. However, I reasoned that if other comedians were going to steal my routines, I had better perform them myself or I would never be paid for any of my material.

When I later recorded the routine, I actually left out the part that Don stole because I didn't want people accusing me of stealing from him! The missing part was the submarine commander talking to his men, and it went something like this:

I'd like to congratulate you men on the teamwork we displayed. We cut a full two minutes off the previous record of four minutes and twenty-nine seconds in surfacing and firing at the target and resubmerging. I just want to congratulate you men on the teamwork. At the same time, I don't want to in any way slight the men that we had to leave on-deck. I think they had a lot to do with the two minutes we cut off the record, and I doubt that any of us will soon forget their somewhat stunned expressions as we watched them through the periscope.

As the years passed and I retold this story, I never used Don's name. But in 2005, Don passed away, and his wife, Dorothy, who always liked the routine, asked me to tell the story at his memorial service, so I did. Everyone there nodded in acknowledgment. They all knew Don. Truthfully, I became philosophical about the whole situation, realizing that I was really indebted to Don for inadvertently causing me to become a performing stand-up.

A few years after Don appropriated my work, I lent a routine to Bill Daily—and I had a devil of a time getting it back. Bill was a friend of mine from Chicago. He I were both trying to break into stand-up at the same time. I had no club dates booked, and he needed material. He was working with a folk singer named Gibson, and he was going to be opening a nightclub in a basement on Chicago Avenue.

Bill was familiar with my routine "The Grace L. Ferguson Airline (And Storm Door Co.)." The routine is about flying on a discount airline that has eliminated a few of the frills and extras, like navigational instruments and maintenance. Bill asked to borrow the routine, and I agreed to lend it to him.

A year later, I was making a follow-up to my album *The Button-Down Mind of Bob Newhart* called, appropriately, *The Button-Down Mind Strikes Back*, and I was one cut short. I phoned Bill and told him that I would have to take back the Grace L. Ferguson routine.

"But that's my strongest bit," he protested feebly.

I resisted saying, "Bill, doesn't that tell you something?" and instead explained that the routine was merely on loan. He was a gentleman about returning it. Obviously, there were no hard feelings because he ended up playing Howard the airline pilot on *The Bob Newhart Show* for six seasons. At least, there weren't any hard feelings on my part.

•

The album *The Button-Down Mind of Bob Newhart* turned out to be bigger than I ever could have dreamed in my wildest imagination. It came about because Dan Sorkin had given some of the early radio tapes I made with Ed Gallagher to George Avakian, director of artists and repertory for Warner Bros. Records. George loved the routines and thought they might make a funny album. When I met with George, he told me to let him know the next time I played in front of an audience so he could send a team of engineers to record the performance. He felt the interplay with the audience would make a much better record than a studio recording.

That sounded fine, but there was one small problem: I had never played a nightclub.

I didn't know the first thing about what I was getting into, so I asked around town about managers. I met with a few and eventually signed with Frank "Tweet" Hogan, who had handled Mike and Elaine and Shelley Berman. Tweet canvassed the country for a club that would book an unknown act. Finally, five months after Warner Bros. made its offer, Tweet booked me as the opening act at the Tidelands Motor Inn in Houston.

For two weeks at the Tidelands, I performed "Abe Lincoln vs. Madison Avenue," "The Driving Instructor," and "The Cruise of the U.S.S. *Codfish*," a.k.a. "The Submarine Commander." None of the routines had titles when I wrote them, but for copyright purposes—and to make the album look somewhat professional—the Warner Bros. record executives assigned titles to them.

I also tried out new material because I only had enough to fill half the album. After the show, I would go back to the hotel with Ken and Mitzi Welch, who were the closing act at the club, and perform the new routines for them. They would listen and tell me which ones were funny enough to test out the next night. From those nights came "The Wright Brothers" and "Nobody Will Ever Play Baseball."

"The Wright Brothers" was a phone conversation between a salesman from a new production corporation and Orville Wright talking about how they would market this new invention called the airplane. "Is there any way of putting a john on it?" the salesman asks. "Jerry came up with an idea I kind of like. Maybe we could set up a little snob appeal–type thing and get two classes, one with a john and one without." The salesman is also worried about travel time. "That's going to cut our time to the Coast if we have to land every 105 feet. . . ."

In "Nobody Will Ever Play Baseball," Abner Double-day tries to sell a game manufacturer on baseball. The manufacturer is skeptical because it takes eighteen people to play. "You see," he tells Abner, "the ideal game is that two or three couples come over to the house and they get a little smashed."

On February 10, 1960, my performance was recorded for my first album, and I became the newest pledge to the fraternity of working stand-up comedians. There was no secret ceremony. I simply went backstage at the end of the night and poured myself a double scotch.

•

Around the time that the album was supposed to be re-leased in April 1960, I called Warners and asked when it was coming out. I couldn't find it any stores in Chicago. They told me that it was already out and that they were shipping every available copy to Minneapolis because it was flying off the shelves there.

I figured that if all else failed at least I could play Fred-die's in Minneapolis for the rest of my life.

Then the album started selling. Everywhere. *The Button-Down Mind* shot to No. 1 on the Billboard record charts, and soon became a true phenomenon. The format was so new that it was called a "spoken-word" album, not a comedy album.

When the record hit, word got back to me from the

neighborhood where I grew up that Louie Jordan, a child-hood friend, proclaimed, "He was always the funniest guy on the corner." Of course, that wasn't exactly a guarantee of success. There are a lot of guys on a lot of corners in Chicago, but I appreciated the acknowledgment.

Warners wanted a sequel immediately, so I wrote some more and recorded *The Button-Down Mind Strikes Back*. I used every available piece of material, including "Bus Driver's School." The second album was released at the end of the year, and it quickly shot up the *Billboard* charts to No. 2, right behind the first album. Just like that, I had the top two albums in the country.

Playboy magazine hailed me "the best new comedian of the decade." Of course, there were still nine more years left in the decade so there was plenty of time to be supplanted.

The culmination of my surreal year came at the 1961 Grammy Awards saluting the best of 1960. I won best new artist of the year, best comedy performance for *The Button-Down Mind Strikes Back*, and album of the year for *The Button-Down Mind*. In the album of the year category, I beat out Frank Sinatra. It just got back to me recently that Frank was mad that he didn't win. Amazing. But then again, it didn't take too much to up-set Frank.

It turns out my two albums held the No. 1 and No. 2 spots for two consecutive weeks. This record stayed in place until the simultaneous release of Guns N' Roses *Use Your Illusion I* and *II* in 1991. When my daughter Jennifer de-livered the news that Axl Rose had supplanted my record, I was philosophical about it. "Well, you hate to lose a record, especially when you don't know you hold it, but at least it went to a friend."

Really, I didn't know I had the record. What good is a record if you don't know you hold it?

Seriously, the sales statistics of my first two albums were impressive. I've read that *The Button-Down Mind* sold more than one million copies and outsold every album made by the Beatles in the sixties. *The Button-Down Mind Strikes Back* sold more than 500,000 copies. However, I've never seen the actual figures. After many years, my representatives and I decided to audit Warner Bros. Records.

And, no, I don't know Axl Rose.

Everyone has probably heard stories about the fuzzy math used in Hollywood accounting. Without getting into the technical minutiae, the big complaint is that the studios deduct "expenses" from profitable films, TV shows, and records before paying the artist's share. These expenses include overhead, which are things like leased BMWs and fuel for the company jet, and marketing costs, such as running the same ad five times in the first half hour of *The Young and the Restless*.

Being a trained accountant, I figured I would have an advantage in the audit.

Not so. There were bigger problems than ledger entries. Warners called back and said with a straight face that the records had been destroyed in a fire. Apparently, the fire was just in the Ns; it didn't touch the Ms or the Os.

Lately, however, I have begun to receive royalties on the albums on a quarterly basis. I'm not exactly sure how they calculate them without all the financial records and contracts that burned up in the Great Warners Office Fire of

'73, but they apparently have a formula. Just last week I received a check for $1.18.

·

Shortly after *The Button-Down Mind* hit the record charts, I was playing the Hungry Eye in San Francisco, and the line wrapped around the block. It seemed that everybody had to see this new comedian. I didn't exactly think of myself as a celebrity, or even a bit celebrity, but I appreciated the attention.

One night during this sold-out, standing-room-only engagement, the stage manager came into my dressing room and told me that Vivien Leigh was in the audience. As if that wasn't enough to make me nervous, he told me that she wanted to come backstage after the show and say hello.

Sure enough, five minutes after the show ended, Scarlett O'Hara was in my dressing room. Having divorced Sir Laurence Olivier, she was with her boyfriend, John Merrivale. The stammer I used in my act suddenly became part of my normal speech.

"Would you care to join us?" she asked me. "We are having a party at the Fairmont Hotel."

"I, uh, I have another show to do . . ." I apologized.

"What time do you get through?"

"Usually about one-thirty in the morning," I confessed, feeling like the janitor who works the night shift.

"That's fine, the party would still be going on," she said, tossing out, "It should be fun. Clifton Webb and George Cukor will be there."

Wow, I thought. I rushed through an abbreviated third

show and caught a cab to the Fairmont. The party was in the presidential suite. For my first true party of movie stars, it immediately impressed. The martini glasses were iced. There was music playing and people were dancing in the middle of the living room.

Vivien Leigh glided over and greeted me. She apologized that George Cukor wasn't feeling well and consequently had turned in early. "He's sorry he missed you," she said.

She introduced me around the room, and I began chatting with some of the guests. Clifton Webb sidled up next to me and introduced himself. Then he asked me if I would like to dance.

As hard as I tried to reverse roles and quickly come up with a line like "my dance card is full," I couldn't. Notwithstanding the fact that he had been a professional ballroom dancer since the age of nineteen, I politely declined. From then on, whenever I saw a Mr. Belvedere picture, my mind would wander back to that time.

•

My other auspicious invitation was from Bob Finkel, the producer of the 1960 Emmy Awards telecast—the *national* Emmy Awards. He called and asked if I could perform my "Abe Lincoln" routine on the show. I was working at Freddie's, so I asked the owner for three days off. Reasoning that my appearance on TV would be good for business, he agreed to extend my run by three days to cover the lost days.

From the moment I arrived at the auditorium for rehearsals, I was in awe. Steve Allen was hosting and his players group, Tom Poston, Don Knotts, and Louie Nye, were all there. In his squeaky voice, and with his head bobbing, Don Knotts walked up and introduced himself to me. I wasn't prepared to be treated like I belonged. As it turned out, I even ended up being called upon for overtime duty.

Mike and Elaine were performing on the show and they wanted to do a routine about shampoo. The producer, Bob Finkel, nixed the idea because Clairol was a major sponsor and they deemed the routine derogatory toward shampoo. When Mike Nichols heard the news, he insisted they were going to do the routine anyway. Told that they absolutely could not, Mike and Elaine walked.

It was the afternoon of the show, and Bob Finkel and the show's head writer, Ed Simmons, came into the makeup room and asked me what else I could do. I volunteered "The Submarine Commander." They asked if it would fit into the theme of the Emmy Awards, which was "television." I performed a version of it for them. Both Bob and Ed, as well as the makeup people, seemed to like it, and they went off to figure out how to fit it into the show's theme.

•

In the wake of the album's release, my brand of humor quickly became synonymous with the "button-down mind." It's a catchy phrase, but I had nothing to do with it. The phrase was concocted by someone in the marketing department of Warner Bros. Records when we were trying to decide on a title. My suggestion was *The Most Celebrated New Comedian Since Attila the Hun*. Though the ad men didn't like my title, they agreed to use it as the sub-title.

So how did they come up with the "button-down mind"?

Four of the routines on the record were about advertising or marketing: "Abe Lincoln vs. Madison Avenue," "Nobody Will Ever Play Baseball," "The Khrushchev Landing Rehearsal," and "Merchandising the Wright Brothers." At the time, the uniform of the day on Madison Avenue was the button-down collar, so someone made the connection and I became synonymous with this ad slogan.

After the album broke, my price for performing stand-up skyrocketed from basically zero to $500 a week. I booked several dates at the new rate. Then I was offered an eye-popping $2,000 a week to play Harrah's in Lake Tahoe. I wondered what the catch was. Do they beat you up between shows? Why in the world would they pay somebody $2,000 to tell jokes as the opening act for Peggy Lee?

No matter; I accepted.

When I arrived, I tracked down the entertainment director to learn the protocol for a stand-up earning two grand as an opening act.

"Am I supposed to gamble part of the money?" I asked. "You know, as a kick . . . a reinvestment in the casino. Because it seems like an awful lot of money."

"No, no, we don't want that at all," he said. "We've had other performers gamble away their paychecks and they do terrible shows because they end up working for noth-

ing. We don't want you to gamble at all, just entertain the
gamblers."

•

With another Chicago winter looming and several choices
brought on by the success of the album, I accepted a six-
week job at the Crescendo in Los Angeles, largely because
I knew the weather would be pleasant. I figured this
whole bubble could burst, so I'd better take advantage of
the sunshine when I could. The job called for me to headline for the first three weeks and to spend the second three
weeks as the opening act for the piano player Errol Garner.

Truthfully, it was always in the back of my mind that
one day I would walk up onstage, nobody would laugh,
and the manager would toss me out into the street. Or
worse, the audience just wouldn't show up, which tells
you, "We know your trick; we're on to your trick."

As I was packing for L.A., I received a phone call asking
if I could come out a day early. A prominent entertainment attorney named Greg Bautzer wanted me to perform
at a private party at his house. He was offering me $1,500
for the night, which is what I was being paid for an entire
week at the Crescendo.

It turned out to be an informal audition to the big time.
I'll never forget standing in the middle of Greg Bautzer's
living room, doing "The Driving Instructor." I looked one
way and there was George Burns. Seated in the back of the
room was Danny Kaye. Up front was Jack Benny. In my in-
security, I was reviewing my performance as I went: *Jack
knows that I am timing this all wrong. . . . Wait, he's laugh-*

ing. . . . He's still laughing. . . . George is laughing, too. . . . Maybe there's hope for me yet.

Jack Benny actually became a fan of mine. He and his wife, Mary Livingstone, and George Burns and Gracie Allen came to the Crescendo to see me one night. I performed "Abe Lincoln vs. Madison Avenue," and Jack loved it. After the show, he came backstage and said, "If I'm ever in the audience, finish the routine you're doing and do 'Abe Lincoln.' "

Years later, I obliged Jack. I was playing the Palmer House in Chicago, and I spotted Jack in the audience. It was my closing night, and he was opening the following night, so his presence wasn't wholly unexpected.

By this time, I had come to feel that "Abe Lincoln" was too long (and thus I've even shortened it for this book). Audiences' attention spans had shrunk, which was largely the result of the quick hit comedy of *Rowan & Martin's Laugh-In*, and I could feel them getting restless during some of my longer routines. My job as a comedian was to adjust to this cultural shift, so I cut "Abe Lincoln" in half.

After the show, Jack appeared backstage and listed everything I had left out. I could fool all of the people some of the time, and some of the people all of the time, but I couldn't fool Jack Benny any of the time.

•

I traveled constantly to take advantage of the offers that were pouring in, living from motel to hotel. I grew tired of looking at phony fruit bowls bolted to the tops of television sets and getting locked out of my room on the way back from the ice machine. The closets all had those hangers with the small hooks that are talking to you, warning, "You don't really think you can take some of these, do you, Bob?" To rail against the system, I thought about stealing fifty or so and then having a small pole installed at home so I could use the hotel hangers.

It's not just the hangers. Everything in the room is accusatory: The sheets and towels have the name of the establishment stamped on them, the pictures are screwed into the walls—usually crooked—and the bathrobes have signs in the pockets that say "Available for purchase at the hotel gift shop." As if I'd steal a used robe.

There was plenty of downtime on the road, and I had difficulty filling it with any productive work. I was beginning to learn that there's a certain satisfaction at the end of a day of having transferred a pile of papers from one side of a desk to the other. In comedy, the papers seem to stay stacked in the same place for days on end.

When it came time to write a new routine, I'd play a game with myself called "The Writing Routine." I'd be sitting in a hotel room, and I'd get mad at myself. "Okay, you're gonna have to write a routine. You haven't written a routine in a while. It's good discipline to sit down and write."

Not so fast. I'd look around the hotel room and realize that I didn't have a legal pad. I only wrote with No. 2 pencils on college-ruled, yellow legal pads. Therefore, I needed to find a stationery store to buy legal pads and pencils, I reasoned.

I would head down to the hotel gift shop and buy a map of the downtown area where I was staying. Back in the room, I would pull out the yellow pages and look for stationery stores. I would match up the addresses to determine which one was closest.

At this point, I would look at my watch. Hmm . . . four o'clock. Well, I'd say to myself, there's no point in trying to do something today because the stationery store is going to be closed by the time I get there.

And then I'd repeat the process the next day.

Dick Martin was much luckier finding material in his travels. He once checked into a hotel that was C-shaped. Shortly after settling into his room, he was looking out the window. On the other side of the building he noticed a man who was by himself in a room and was engaging in what, in polite circles, would be called self-love.

Dick was in room 807. By counting along the building, Dick quickly figured out the man was in room 842. He picked up the phone, dialed the man's room, and watched.

The man answered the phone with a curt "Who is this?"

Dick replied, "This is God, cut it out."

•

One thing I've learned since winning my three Grammies is that in the entertainment business, awards are only one way in which success is measured.

My first brush with this came in 1970. I had a small part in the film *On a Clear Day You Can See Forever,* which was directed by Vincente Minnelli and starred Barbra Streisand. As was customary, the billing of the actors had been settled up front. But after the movie was finished, the producers came to me and said that Jack Nicholson, who also had a small part in the film, had been nominated for an Oscar for *Five Easy Pieces.* They asked if they could bill him above me, despite the fact that it was in breach of my contract. I told them that if Jack *won* the Oscar, they could bill him ahead of me. He didn't.

I've never measured success by awards. In fact, I think the whole awards-giving process needs rethinking. For starters, they should bestow lifetime achievement awards at the beginning of a performer's career. This way the person can still enjoy it while he is young, rather than giving it to him when he has lost most of his marbles and is standing onstage wondering why all these overdressed people are applauding.

If the performer had a lousy career, they could take back the lifetime achievement award. They would have a taking-back ceremony, where luminaries would say things like, "I thought he was a shoo-in to be successful" and "I gave him his first lead role and he just killed the movie." Stripping a performer of an important award after a long career sounds cruel, but it's not. Since the taking-back ceremony would happen in the performer's dotage, he wouldn't really understand what was happening.

In a way, I'm lucky I don't have four Emmys like, say, Kelsey Grammer. My wife, Ginnie, feels that if you openly display trophies, you are bragging. I think most women feel this way. You hear the stories all the time. A guy goes out and risks his life hunting elk, and his wife won't let him hang the stuffed head over the fireplace.

I've found ways to cheat this rule for the most important of accolades—but only barely. My Grammys for *The Button-Down Mind* are discreetly placed on a bookshelf in the den. For years, my daughter Courtney thought they were bookends from a yard sale.

On prominent display is the Mark Twain Prize for humor given to me by the Kennedy Center—and, Ginnie,
sweetheart, I'm quoting here—"to honor the brilliant
minds that elbow American culture to see if it's still alive."
This one is on the coffee table, where it will stay until
Ginnie moves it. Which she does once a year to make room
for the Christmas decorations.

*

I've found that there's no real comfort in success. There's
never time to slow down, sit back, and relax. But there did
come a moment later in my career when I knew that I had
truly made it as a comedian.

After I presented Richard Pryor with the lifetime
achievement award at the American Comedy Awards, we
were backstage posing for pictures. He looked up at me
and said, "I stole your album."

For a split second, I couldn't believe what I was hearing.
The great Richard Pryor stealing my material? I was honored and stunned at the same time.

"In Peoria, I went into the record store and I put it under my jacket and I walked out," he continued.

"Richard, I get a quarter royalty on every album."

With that, Richard Pryor pulled out a quarter and
handed it to me.

To have your album stolen by Richard Pryor is quite an
achievement.

Barreling down the Outer Drive, McGee thought he spotted his stolen car in the adjacent lane. He sped up and crowded the car. Ed, having no idea what was going on, became concerned. "You're getting a little close . . ."

When McGee was certain the car was his, he bumped the fender to run the driver off the road. Ed crouched down in horror. "You just bumped the guy!"

McGee then swerved into the car and forced it onto the grass. By this time, Ed was under the dashboard in a state of shock. The two guys in the car jumped out and ran. McGee took another look at the car and mumbled, "That's not my car."

Boxing with McGee involved going to the Oak Park YMCA twice a week. They had a makeshift boxing ring of canvas spread over tumbling mats and surrounded by sagging ropes.

One day we were sparring and I stepped backward and caught my foot on the canvas. I fell forward, totally defenseless, and he hit me. He didn't knock me out, but I landed facedown on the canvas.

"Why did you do that?" I asked him.

"I've never seen an opening like that," he said gleefully.

I decided it was time to learn how to box, so I asked Jimmy Sheeran, the Loyola boxing team member, to teach me.

Jimmy and I met at the Northwestern gym, which was a couple of blocks from the Loyola campus, and practiced leading and defending. We wore gloves, but our hands weren't wrapped and we didn't use mouthpieces or headgear.

This continued for two or three sessions, and one day we began sparring. Jimmy unexpectedly whapped me in the

> 〉 〉 〉 〉 〉

CHAPTER SIX

Dying Onstage
Isn't That Painful

When I was a student at Loyola University, there was a guy in my class named Jimmy Sheeran. He was on the Loyola boxing team, which has since been discontinued. I was a huge boxing viewer. Every Wednesday night, my friend Jack Galley and I watched *Pabst Blue Ribbon Bouts* on TV. I planned my entire day around it. I would go over to his house and watch because he had a television set and we didn't have one at that time. He was middle class.

Another friend of mine named Jim McGee, a colorful and unpredictable character, was also an amateur boxer. Even though he outweighed me by twenty pounds, he asked me to train with him.

One time, when both he and my friend Ed Gallagher worked downtown, McGee was in his car and passed Ed on the street. He offered to give him a lift, Ed hopped in, and McGee started driving north on the Loop. Though Ed didn't know it, McGee was driving a loaner car because his car had been stolen.

head. Reasoning that the rules of our training had changed, I whapped him back. We began punching each other, leading and defending. You know, really boxing.

From time to time, other guys would wander by Jimmy and me boxing and ask if they could try it. We said, "Sure," and asked, "Which one?" They would look at Jimmy's face and my face and invariably choose me.

During our sessions Jimmy gave me a deviated septum, probably from a left hook. I didn't think much of it at the time until my induction physical, when the doctor said, "Bend over," which I did, and the doctor said, "How did you get the deviated septum?" and I wondered, "You can see it from there?"

The reason I bring this whole subject up is that when I perform stand-up and the audience either doesn't laugh or heckles me, I think to myself, "I can get through this because at least nobody is hitting me in the face."

•

There isn't a comedian in show business who hasn't tanked onstage. In a strange way it becomes funny when you're halfway through the show, you've done your best material, you know you don't have anything stronger coming up, and no one is laughing. You just want to hang yourself.

I experienced this sinking feeling in my second appearance ever, at the Elmwood Casino in Windsor, Ontario. My record hadn't yet been released, so no one knew who I was. The crowd was very polite. They didn't boo. They just kept eating their dinner. I knew it wasn't working, so it became funny in a perverse sort of way. All I could do was press on.

The club was a real throwback. They had a line of chorus

girls, an Italian singer, and a dumbbell act. Actually, the dumbbell act was fascinating. They were two Italian brothers who didn't speak any English. After all, you don't have to say much if you are in a dumbbell act, you just throw the dumbbells back and forth, catch them between your legs or behind your back, and then bow.

The dumbbell act had a big closing number. The emcee would call somebody from the audience onto the stage, and the volunteer would sit on a chair between the dumbbell throwers. They would put a cigarette in the person's mouth, and then stand five feet away on either side of the chair, and throw the dumbbells behind the volunteer's head. For the grand finale, they would knock the cigarette out of the person's mouth.

Sometimes they knocked the cigarette out, other times they cut it too close and hit the unsuspecting audience member in the side of the head. Let me tell you, when they creased the volunteer with the dumbbell, the routine just fell apart.

The chorus girls would come out and dance for a few minutes, and then it was my turn. I took the stage and performed for about twenty minutes. For whatever reason, the Canadian audience wasn't taking to my act. I would leave the stage, and the dancers would return.

This went on for four consecutive nights. Sometimes the Italian dumbbell throwers would knock out the cigarette, other times they would hit the volunteer in the head. The girls would dance, I would do my act to a lukewarm response, and the dancers would close the show. On the fifth night, I did about fourteen minutes and I died, so I cut things short, thanked the audience, and left the stage.

As I walked backstage, I passed the girls' dressing room where they were changing. I heard someone say, "Holy S---, he's off!"

The manager of the Elmwood walked up to me. In a thick German accent, he said to me, *"Jou have to do eighteen meanuts."*

"I did fourteen minutes and it didn't work, so I know that, uh, another four minutes is not going to work," I explained. "I don't have any stronger material."

"Jou need to do eighteen meanuts.... The girls needs eighteen meanuts to change costumes."

Just when I was feeling totally deflated that my entire act was to facilitate the dancers' costume change, the club owner walked up to me. His name was Al, and he was in the jukebox business in Canada. He patted me on the back. "I own the Blue Room in Toronto," he said. "I'd like you to play it sometime."

"Th-thank you," I stammered, thinking to myself that this guy was some kind of sadist who got his kicks from watching comedians die every night on stage. For a minute, I considered returning to accounting.

•

Dan Rowan and Dick Martin were famous for how they handled unruly audiences. These two comedians were basically one brain because each always knew what the other was thinking.

Once they were playing a hotel in Kansas City and virtually everyone in the crowd was drunk and disorderly. People were talking and yelling over the jokes, so Dan said, "We are now going to take you to the site of the 1954

Olympics. I'll be talking to the world's fastest man, and he will describe to me what thoughts are going through his mind."

Dan and Dick got down on all fours and ran off the stage, through the audience, out of the auditorium, and into an elevator. They didn't stop until they were in their rooms. Meanwhile, the audience craned their necks and collectively went through the thought process of: "I wonder where they went. . . . I guess they're coming back. . . . They're coming back, aren't they?"

I've certainly had my fair share of hecklers over the years. I had a heckler at my first nightclub appearance, and she nearly torpedoed my entire career.

It was two weeks into my run at the Tidelands, and the Warner team arrived to record my show for what became *The Button-Down Mind.* I did two shows a night, which gave me two shots at the recording.

I took the stage for the first show and began doing my routines. As if I wasn't nervous enough, there was a woman in the front row who kept saying, "That's a bunch of crap." There was an odd rhythm to the show. During each pause in the routines, she'd blurt out, "That's a bunch of crap." After the show, we listened to the tape. Her voice was much clearer than mine.

Luckily, she thought my act was such a bunch of crap that she didn't stay for the second show.

Though each heckler really needs to be handled on a case-by-case basis, I have developed a few reliable retorts. The two most basic:

"Look, sir, I don't come down in the sewer and bother you at work, so why are you bothering me?" and "I'll tell you what. I'll check my brains at the door and we'll start off even."

At nightclubs, particularly in the sixties and seventies, the booze really flowed, so I encountered many a drunken heckler. Typically it was after midnight and some guy who had had a few too many mai tais would be trying to impress his girlfriend. In these cases, I used the girlfriend and predicted what might happen to him after the show.

"Sir, the way you are acting I don't think you're going to get any tonight."

"I can hear your lady after the show: 'Well, you certainly made an ass of yourself tonight.' "

An airplane flying overhead elicits a standard, "Pull up! Pull up!" With a circling helicopter, I go further: "I didn't see the news today. Are we under attack?"

But the biggest problem I've had was dealing with a heckler in the middle of a routine. "The Submarine Commander" would be well under way and I'd get heckled. I would have to go out of character to put him down, unless I could do some fancy footwork and somehow work the put-down into the routine. Such as: "Sailor, I'll deal with you in a minute," or "Johnson, why are you always so much trouble?"

If I'm performing a telephone routine, I can usually weave something in. During "King Kong," for instance, I'll say, "I'll deal with you in a minute, sir. . . . Sorry, sir, someone had a question about whether the elevators go all the way to the top. I told him these elevators do, but clearly his doesn't." Another standard phone routine retort: "He did appear to be a little drunk, yes, sir."

The only way to save a routine is to stay in the moment

so the audience doesn't lose its train of thought. Otherwise, I have to break character to put the heckler down and then start the routine over. If I have to stop for more than a sentence or two, I've lost the momentum. That really used to frustrate me, which is why I favored colleges over nightclubs. At colleges, there aren't many hecklers. At least there weren't before "Hi, Bob."

•

Perversity is an innate trait in comedians, and dealing with dumb audiences requires perversity. When you face a dumb audience, it's worse than being heckled because they just sit there and stare at you. One particular evening, I was in a certain city on the East Coast that had the slowest audience, and I decided to fight back.

"I guess people probably wonder what comedians do during the day because we travel a lot and have downtime before the show," I began. "Well, I happen to belong to the Road Runner Club. It's quite interesting and very well organized. We have different chapters in each city. One thing we do is that we get together and we talk about our favorite Road Runner cartoon. . . ."

As I looked out over a sea of confused faces waiting for something funny to emerge, I wondered how far I could take this. What the hell, I thought, I'm feeling a little crazy. For them, I'll take it a little farther.

"Yesterday, we were talking about my favorite episode, the one where Wile E. Coyote is chasing the Road Runner . . . or maybe it was Bugs Bunny who was chasing him. I forget now. Anyway, Bugs Bunny gets hold of a can of paint, and he paints a tunnel on the rock. Remember that one?"

Blank stares.

Here's another. I'll set it up by saying, "There are certain victimless crimes that police have to spend their time on, like gambling. You aren't hurting anybody."

And then I'll move into the joke. "All of the guys in the audience, we've all done this. The wife and kids are out of the house. You are all alone, and you slip on one of the wife's dresses. You aren't hurting anybody."

At this point, there is a long delay with no response from the audience. "You mean . . . you don't do that?"

No one ever laughs at these bits. They might be a little bit perverse, but sometimes the audience deserves it. There are plenty of small, twisted things that I've left in my act over the years just because I felt like it.

In "Introducing Tobacco to Civilization," there's a line where the head of the West Indies Company is talking to Sir Walter Raleigh, who is telling him about discovering tobacco. The company man says, "You see, Walt, we've been a little worried about you ever since you put your cape down over that mud."

That never gets a laugh. People usually stop laughing just to try to figure out the reference. Most people don't remember that one of the famous stories about Sir Walter Raleigh was that he took off his coat and draped it over a mud puddle so a woman disembarking from a carriage wouldn't soil her shoes. When I first performed the routine, people laughed. Over time it has become an obscure reference, and today almost no one makes the connection.

The fictitious names Larry Strickland and Neal Norlag are another laugh-stopper. In "The Bus Driver's School," I point out that we are going to find out whether the students will be good bus drivers, or possibly some of the all-time great bus drivers—bus drivers like the legendary Larry Strickland, or probably that greatest bus driver of all, Neal Norlag. (Remember him?)

It's the bus driver's version of comparing Babe Ruth and Willie Mays. Who was the greatest? They never played at the same time, so we'll never know.

Why not take it out of the routine?

Perversity.

And, incidentally, the Elmwood Casino is named after the elmwood, a type of Canadian flower.

•

It wasn't until years later when I met Harpo Marx that I began to understand how truly great comedians dealt with failure onstage. Ginnie and I were in Palm Springs, and Harpo introduced himself to me and invited us over to his house.

Harpo was an incredibly humble and generous man. He and his wife couldn't have children so they adopted six kids.

We were sitting in his den, and he opened one of his scrapbooks. He pointed out a column outside a vaudeville house. The column had metal plates on it with the names of several performers, including the Marx brothers.

I was curious. "Of all the vaudeville houses that you played in, why did you keep this particular picture?" I asked.

"Because we were there an entire week and we never got a laugh."

The funny thing about comedians is that you will never hear them say, "I killed 'em last night" or "I had 'em rolling in the aisles." What they will say are things like "it was the worst crowd ever," "the whole act went into the dumper," or "I played this club the other night and ... nothing."

Maybe it's comedians' twisted sense of the world, but we remember our worst routines word for word. This can be a little disconcerting because for every routine that works, there seem to be four that don't. For all you sadists out there:

A civilian goes to Mars. When he returns to Earth, he's being interviewed on his impressions of Mars. The interviewer asks if the people on Mars are more advanced than people on Earth. The civilian says they are, and the interviewer asks by how much.

"I would say six, seven weeks," the civilian replies. "When I was up there, they had the disposable razor blades and it was like six or seven weeks after I returned to Earth before we had them."

That was one that died, but I still love it.

•

There was once a comedy team named Brown and Carney. The entertainment business is always looking for the next big thing, and the suits at RKO thought that Wally Brown and Alan Carney could become another Abbott and Costello. This is the kind of delusional thinking that goes on every day in Hollywood. Inevitably, it turned out that Brown and Carney were no Abbott and Costello.

One day they arrived at a vaudeville house just in time for their show. There was no time to rehearse. They handed their sheet music to the band and took the stage. What they didn't know was that the previous act was a poodle act with jugglers that used the exact same music.

The minute the band struck up the music, the poodles ran out onstage and began doing pirouettes. Brown and Carney spent the entire show fighting off the poodles.

I've never been attacked by poodles, but there have been times when things didn't go well due to circumstances slightly beyond my control. The Australians had been after me for years to play Sydney. I had declined because of the long flights. But after turning down a number of offers, I decided to steel myself for the twenty-two hours of flying. When I arrived at the club for the first night's show, I asked the maître d' how many people we were expecting.

"Tonight," he pondered aloud, as he carefully consulted his master list, "we have . . . fourteen."

Wow. Figuring that maybe Monday was an off-night, I asked about the following night.

"Tomorrow, we have nine."

"Wednesday?"

"We don't have any for Wednesday."

Apparently, my *Button-Down Mind* album had cooled off.

That same trip, I was playing a hall in front of 300 people, but it might as well have been empty. Bit after bit, joke after joke, routine after routine, there was nothing but dead air.

"Artie," I said into the microphone, calling to my manager who was in the lighting booth.

Artie came out of the booth. "Yeah, Bob," he said over the silent crowd.

"How much time do I have to do?"

"You have to do an hour."

"An hour? . . . How much time have I done?"

"Thirty-five minutes, Bob."

"Artie, let me know when I've done another twenty-four minutes."

The audience sat stone-silent, watching this exchange. It didn't matter because I wasn't coming back to Australia. Ever.

Sad to say, the situation could've turned out even worse.

Jack Paar used to tell a story about maestro violinist Jascha Heifetz. He gets a call in March from a club owner in North Dakota who wants to book him in November. It sounds like a pretty good gig. The hall holds 3,000. Jascha consults his schedule and agrees.

But come November, there is a terrible blizzard in New York, so Jascha calls the club owner and explains that all the flights have been canceled and he will not be able to make it. The club owner tells Jascha that there are 3,000 people who will be heartbroken if he doesn't show up. Jascha vows to do whatever he can.

After hours on the phone, Jascha finds a flight from La-Guardia that connects through Denver to North Dakota. He finally arrives at the auditorium at 11 P.M., and there are only twelve people there.

He's utterly deflated. "I thought you said there were three thousand," Jascha says to the club owner.

"There were, but they didn't think you were going to show up so they all left," the club owner responds. "But these people have been here since five P.M."

"I've never appeared in front of such a small audience," Jascha says.

"Jascha, it will really make their night if you just sing one or two songs."

Worse than having no one at all or no one laughing was the time that I had a full house and my hair fell off in the middle of the show.

I was appearing at the Palmer House in Chicago and the room was unusually hot. All of a sudden, I felt my hairpiece starting to slip. The glue that held it to my slightly bald spot was apparently melting. As the hairpiece slid down the side of my face, it picked up speed. At the last second, just before it hit the floor, I grabbed it and stuffed it into the pocket of my tuxedo.

The audience was laughing—laughing uneasily, I might add.

"Well, now you know I wear a hairpiece," I said.

This was a great-looking hairpiece, and I used to wear it everywhere I performed. It wasn't one of those bad hairpieces where people say, "Do you really expect me to believe that's your hair? It looks like a dead animal fell out of a tree and landed on your head." Thanks to master craftsmanship, this hairpiece blended with my normal hair perfectly.

Since the rug had been literally pulled back, I worked the situation into the show. An embarrassment of that magnitude demanded that I get some comedic mileage out of it. Every time I put my hand in my pocket, I'd jerk it back out and screech, *"Ay, yi, yi!"* as if I were being bitten.

The audience loved it. They knew they were witnessing something that, hopefully for my sake, the next audience wouldn't see.

•

In the early seventies, I filled in for Johnny Carson as guest host of *The Tonight Show* from New York. He was having contractual problems with NBC—which meant that he wanted more money. NBC's stance was that Johnny wasn't going to hold them up for any more money no matter what. (Guess who won?)

This was before *The Bob Newhart Show*, which is to say that it was a pretty big opportunity for me. *The Tonight Show* had a writing staff that was available to help the guest host write the nightly monologue. Each night, they would give me three lousy jokes. Having fulfilled their obligation, they would return to working on their screenplays. With Johnny gone, there wasn't much anyone could do about it.

It fell to me to write the monologues. Each night after the show, I would gather all the New York papers and search for material. Then I would fall asleep skimming the dossier on the following day's guest. After three weeks, I felt like a wet and worn-out dishrag. When Johnny left, he had done it for thirty years.

The one night I thought would go well didn't. My first guest was Bobby Morse, who had starred in the movie version of *How to Succeed in Business Without Really Trying*.

Bobby was a friend of mine, but the problem turned out to be that we knew each other's stories. Everything fell flat. Nothing worked. The poor audience who had gotten their tickets six months in advance to see Johnny were watching Bobby Morse and me tank. It was so silent that you could hear the air conditioner.

Finally the segment ended, and we went to commercial. I had never been so relieved. I knew the segment bombed, but at least it was over. Next up was an organ player. During the three-minute commercial break, the stagehands wheeled out the organ. They plugged in the organ and smoke began billowing from the top.

"Bob," the producer said, "do another slug with Bobby."

And so we did.

When the torture finally ended, Ed McMahon chimed in, "Have you two ever considered writing a book?"

•

I used to love to sit home at night and watch Johnny go down in flames. There was nothing better.

John—it's hard to call him Johnny—became a good friend of mine over the years. I hosted the show dozens of times. For a while, we were neighbors at the beach.

My fondest memories are from the seventies. After doing the show, John, Ed McMahon, Doc Severinsen, me, and all of our wives would go to a little joint on Sunset called Sneaky Pete's and unwind. After last call, we would all come back to my house and laugh it up.

One night when John and I were playing the drums in my den, Ginnie announced that she needed to go upstairs and go to bed because she had to wake up early to take the kids to school.

The following day, John bought an old army cot and had it delivered to the house. The note read: "For Mrs. Newhart." So she could sleep downstairs.

There was a devilish side to Johnny, but he wasn't cruel. On the air, he wouldn't put an ingénue starring in the latest romantic comedy on the spot. He would only try to befuddle people he knew could handle it. He knew that I would go along with him. He trusted me, and he would never let me look bad.

But he loved to push me to the edge. He loved to toss out a random question that wasn't in the pre-interview, such as, "Do you ever ski?" and I'd have to pick it up from there. First, I'd give him a look: you sonofabitch.

Once, when I filled in at the last minute for Dennis Hopper, Johnny asked me the questions prepared for Dennis Hopper. I knew right away where he was going.

Him: "What was your favorite experience making a movie?"

Me: "I'd have to say *Easy Rider*, at least the part I remember of it. I was so bombed during filming that I've forgotten a lot of it."

It took the audience a while, but they caught on.

•

I wasn't opposed to returning the favor, and I once did. It came during the time when Johnny's show aired for an hour and a half.

During these years, the last guest would be a writer or author of some kind. I was usually the first guest, so I would come out and have my exchange with Johnny and then move down one seat on the couch. After the second guest finished, he would take my seat and I would move further down the couch. Ed was always at the end, next to a table that held a faceless clock used by Johnny to determine how long it was until the end of the show.

One night, the author guest was particularly boring. During the author's segment, I was sitting next to Ed. Whenever Johnny looked away, I motioned to Ed to move the clock back five minutes. As Johnny's exchange with the author grew more and more boring, Johnny glanced at the clock. Each time he would get a weird expression on his face that seemed to say, "There can't possibly be twenty more minutes left." Finally, at the point when Johnny thought that there were still fifteen minutes left, producer Freddy DeCordova gave the signal and Doc played the *Tonight Show* theme.

There was no friendly retribution from Johnny for this—though the next time I appeared on *The Tonight Show* I noticed that they had put a glass face over the clock so no one could change the time.

•

On the night of November 15, 1990, Johnny's monologue died, and I was his first guest. I knew from his sly introduction, in which he weaved together the facts that I was the voice of Bernard the Mouse in *The Rescuers Down Under* and the grand marshal of the Rose Parade, that I was in trouble. So after I was introduced and the curtain opened, I stayed put. I wanted Johnny to think, just for a second, that I might not come out.

Of course, I did. Here's our exchange:

I said, "This is important to me. I don't have a show anymore. I don't have a check coming in every week. I've got to score here tonight or it could all be over."

"It can't all be over when you're Bernard the Mouse. The bidding for your services must have been incredible ... Bernard the Mouse and the grand marshal ... I know you were back there screaming your head off, watching me die," Johnny said.

"That's right, nobody does it better," I said.

"You've had these nights—"

"Not really, no. ... It's quite an honor to be the grand marshal. Frank Sinatra was the grand marshal. Gregory Peck was the grand marshal. I'm only the third comedian to be grand marshal, aside from politicians. I was amazed when I saw the list of grand marshals that your name was not among them. ... I've always considered you a much bigger star than I am."

"The reason was that they probably caught me on a night like tonight and said, 'Maybe we should forget that man and call Newhart.' "

"It could have been the 'D' word."

"Sinatra remarried and he was the grand marshal."

"That's true," I said. "My theory is out the window. I guess they just never thought of you. ... Were you offered?"

"My schedule is so busy here I probably wouldn't have had time to go over there anyway. ... What is the theme of the parade this year, blinking? ... They usually have a theme."

"Yes, they have a theme. It's called fun and games, and I am the fun."

"I know you are riding in the parade, and you have to get up quite early—"

"There are a number of duties."

"What are the duties? This I wouldn't know, having never been asked to—"

"That's amazing. . . . Really."

"I know it is."

"You have to attend various functions, and you have to have your picture taken with the Rose Bowl queen, who is a very beautiful young girl."

"Who is the Rose Bowl queen?"

Here I drew a blank. "Sorry, uh . . ."

"Aren't you the grand marshal?"

"I am the grand marshal, and we had pictures taken the other day . . ."

"Who is the Rose Bowl queen?"

"Apparently you think it's fun to make fun of someone in the advanced stages of Alzheimer's. . . ."

"You are going for the sympathy routine. . . . It's understandable, you are in for a quickie picture. It probably just escaped your mind."

"And some of the other duties. I ride in the float and wave for about three miles. You flip the coin for two teams—and you get to keep the coin. . . . It's quite an honor."

"It is. . . . That's all there is to it?"

"That's quite a bit, really."

"This goes to many countries all over the world."

"Over three hundred million people will see this."

"My goodness . . ."

"You know, envy doesn't become you," I said. "If the tables had been reversed, I would have said how thrilled I was for you."

"Sure, and I would've known who the Rose Bowl queen was."

Johnny took a commercial break and then we finished up on my being the grand marshal of the Rose Bowl Parade.

"I feel terrible," I began. "I was going to look up the name of the queen, but then I said to myself, 'He'll never ask that, so why look it up?' I didn't know that the monologue was going to go into the dumper and once again the captain of the ship was taking the crew down with him."

"That's the way it works."

•

Through all the appearances on *The Tonight Show*, Ginnie and I became good friends with Janet and Freddy DeCordova. Freddy's previous claim to fame was directing Ronald Reagan in *Bedtime for Bonzo*, which Johnny continually kidded him about.

Then, through Janet and Freddy, we met and became good friends with the legendary agent Irving Lazar and his wife, Mary. We spent many wonderful evenings being regaled by their fascinating accounts of Hollywood in the forties and fifties. I miss those times with them,

CHAPTER SEVEN

You Can Get Out of This

Buddy Hackett and I were backstage at a charity event in Los Angeles, waiting to go on and perform our respective routines.

"You're Catholic, right?" Buddy asked me.

"Yes, Buddy. I'm Catholic. Born and raised," I said.

I waited for the punch line, but Buddy took things in a different direction. "I got a girl for you," he said. "She's Catholic. The two of you belong together. I'm gonna fix you up with her."

Her name was Virginia Quinn—Ginnie—and it turned out that she knew something about the entertainment business. A college student at the time, she was working as an extra at Paramount, a pretty typical part-time job in Los Angeles. Her father, Bill Quinn, was a well-known actor. But my newfound fame as a comedian with the No. 1 and No. 2 albums on the *Billboard* charts didn't matter much to her. She had never heard of me.

On our first date, I took her out to dinner. I had already

eaten, so I told her to go ahead and eat. I ordered a drink and watched her eat dinner. She dripped mayonnaise on her purple dress, which, of course, I didn't notice.

She thought my behavior was strange, but it seemed normal to me at the time. Being a comedian, I didn't have the manners back then that I have now.

After dinner, I told her we were going to Carl Reiner's house. Mel Brooks was going to be there. The two of them had written and recorded *The 2000 Year Old Man*, and they were going to play it for us. Instead of being excited, Ginnie said, "You didn't tell me we were going to someone's house." I guess I forgot.

The night went well enough that we began dating, though I'm sad to report not exclusively. The relationship didn't seem to be going anywhere. On my birthday, she gave me an ID bracelet for a present and said, "I want you to have this, but I'm seeing someone else." So we broke up.

Buddy called a few days later and invited me to a party with a bunch of nurses. I declined. Knowing how Buddy's mind worked, I was sure that Ginnie was invited to this alleged nurse party, so I called her and told her about Buddy's ploy. It turned out that Ginnie wasn't going to the party—maybe it really was going to be a roomful of nurses—but she suggested we get together and talk.

Ginnie came over to my apartment, and we talked out the issues. Afterward, we were walking to the market to buy some food so she could cook us dinner. I mentioned that I had a performance coming up in St. Louis and asked her if she would like to come with me.

"You know, you missed the last trip and we almost

didn't make it as a couple, so this might be a good idea," I said. "What do you think?"

"My parents would never let me go with you to St. Louis," she said.

"What if you had a ring?"

"Are you saying what I think you're saying?" she asked.

That's what you call the minimalist proposal. The next day, we picked out an engagement ring for her and made it official.

On January 12, 1963, we made it to the altar. As we took our places, before the procession began, character actor Joe Flynn took one look at Ginnie's dad and quipped, "Look who they got to play the father."

That wasn't as bad as the last thing my soon-to-be father-in-law whispered to his daughter before walking her down the aisle. "Sweetheart," he said, "I can still get you out of this."

But the biggest hurdle of the day was yet to come.

After the reception, Ginnie and I climbed into our car to drive away from the country club as our friends waved to us. I dreaded this moment because, despite the fact that I was thirty-two years old, I still didn't have a driver's license.

Once I became a working comedian, I was on the road forty or fifty weeks a year, so there was no reason to buy a car and let it sit in a garage. When I traveled to a performance, I always stayed in a hotel near the venue and took cabs around so I didn't have to rent a car. Even when I finally moved to Los Angeles, with the crisscrossing ribbons of freeways, I managed to get around town with a combination of public transportation and catching rides with friends.

However, I knew that it would look silly if the bride drove the groom away from the church, so as we walked out of the reception, I told Ginnie that I was going to drive. I put the bride in the passenger side of the car and then climbed behind the wheel of my T-Bird—a car she had encouraged me to buy.

I imagined what I *thought* it would be like driving a car. Like Mrs. Webb had been taught by Frank Dexter in "The Driving Instructor," I checked my rearview mirror. Slowly, I pulled away from the country club, basically driving in a straight line. After two blocks, I stopped the car. Ginnie and I switched places, and she drove us back to our apartment.

In the coming months, I began to test the roadways. I never had a driving instructor. Ginnie helped out, but trial and error was my main teacher. I never used the freeways or the main boulevards like Sunset and Wilshire. Traveling long distances was difficult, but I found backstreets. I would stick with the local streets to slowly build up my confidence. Stop signs were my best friends. Basically, my rule of thumb was to keep it under 20 m.p.h. After a year, I was ready. At age thirty-three, I drove to the DMV, passed the driving test, and got my license.

•

I was educated by the Jesuits. When you are educated by the Jesuits, you are supposed to be intelligent. If that's true, then the most intelligent thing I ever did was marry my wife, Ginnie.

For the past forty-three years, we've had a pretty smooth marriage as those things go. Like all couples, we've had fights, but they never last long. I've found that fights in marriage are generally about something other than the topic you are arguing over.

Ginnie and I had our first fight over thumbtacks. We were newlyweds, and I was helping her line some drawers. This was in the days before sticky paper, so the drawer paper had to be anchored with thumbtacks. Shortly into the project, I informed Ginnie that I was out of thumbtacks.

"How could you be out of them?" she asked.

"Well, I don't have any more. That's how I'm out of them."

"What do you mean? We've done the same amount of drawers and I haven't used all of mine," she said, holding up her allotment.

"I put six in each drawer, one in each corner and two in the middle to hold the paper down."

"Bob, you should only use four in each drawer."

We didn't talk for the next three days.

They say love is blind, and it probably is. When you are engaged, you see these little funny things about your future wife that you think are so cute. From time to time, Ginnie's parents would ask her to do something that she thought wasn't reasonable and she would get her back up and refuse to do it. In those pre-matrimony days, I thought it was pretty cute. The more they would try to push her to do it, the cuter her resistance became.

But eventually you come to grips with all these little traits and see them for what they are. Years later when Ginnie would refuse to do something, I would sit back and think, "You are the most stubborn woman I've ever seen in my life."

Another thing I've learned over the course of marriage is that women argue a lot differently than men. In the case of my marriage, it's magnified. I'm a Virgo, and we're very logical. Ginnie is a Sagittarius, and they tend to be more emotional. Perhaps this is why Ginnie and I once had a fight over something that never happened.

I woke up one morning and greeted her with a "Hi, sweetheart."

She didn't respond. Right away I could see that she was angry. I did what all men do—an instant replay of yesterday. Let's see. I got up. I complimented her on breakfast. I picked up my clothes and put them in the hamper. I spent the day on the golf course with the guys, and so on. I couldn't find any obvious failings.

"You're mad. . . . What's wrong?" I asked.

"I had a dream that we went to a party and you spent the entire party talking to this beautiful young lady."

"Honey," I protested. "That was a dream."

"Yeah, but it's just the kind of thing you would do."

The most serious problem we ever had came just after we were first married. I returned home from work one day, and Ginnie tartly informed me that the mail was waiting on my desk. I went into the spare bedroom in our apartment that doubled as my office to see what was wrong.

There was a letter from a woman who lived in Colorado. It began: "Dear Bob. I'm sorry I couldn't take your advice. I went ahead and had our child and I named him Bob."

Ginnie was mad because she thought it was something

I should have told her about before we got married. Calmly, while frantically showing her my travel logs for the past several years to prove that I hadn't been anywhere near Colorado, I explained that I didn't know this looney-tune lady and that this tryst never happened.

I'm pretty sure Ginnie believed me at the time, but after really getting to know me over the last four decades, I'm sure she believes me now.

•

As in every marriage, my wife has tried to change my behavior for the better over the years, ridding me of bad habits and instilling in me the manners that help me function in polite society. Clothing, for example.

It's hardly an understatement to say, I've never been a clotheshorse. I simply wake up, put on what's comfortable, and go about my day. If I'm doing a TV show or a movie, it's even easier because the wardrobe person tells me what to wear. In *Legally Blonde 2: Red, White & Blonde*, I played a doorman, so I wore a doorman's outfit. In *Elf*, I wore a green elf's costume with a tall, pointy hat. And so on.

But with Ginnie it's different. We'll be getting ready to go to a party. I'll slip on a dark blue cardigan, some royal blue slacks, a yellow-striped shirt, and a pair of gray socks. It used to go like this:

Her: "Bob, you aren't going out like that, are you? That's a joke, right? You're just telling me you don't want to go."

Me: "What are you talking about?"

Her: "The way you're dressed. That's a joke. You aren't really going to go out that way."

Me: "What's wrong?"

Her: "Those colors don't even come close to going together."

Me: "Oh, really? I had no idea."

I'm not color-blind. I just have no eye for what goes with what. So after a while, I changed my tack. Now, it goes more like this:

Her: "Bob, you aren't going out like that, are you?"

Me: "No, of course not. I was just waiting for you to tell me what to wear."

Ginnie's dad had a great theory about clothes. He'd say, "You should always look like you don't need the work." He was a fastidious dresser, and when he'd go to casting calls, he would wear his finest suits. The message was, if I don't get the job, no big deal. I don't need the money.

To heck with that—I'll take the money.

Ginnie also changed our entire family's behavior. We were never ones to tell each other "I love you" when we hung up the phone or said good-bye. She always did, and we began to pick up on this. When my mother was in a nursing home in her later years, my sister Mary Joan would visit her. When she left, she would tell Mom that she loved her. That's a nice habit for any family to get into.

•

Despite the craziness of show business, with all the traveling and odd working hours, Ginnie always tried to maintain some semblance of a normal lifestyle when our kids were growing up. Even when I was performing for four and five weeks at a time in Las Vegas, she would pack up the kids on Fridays after school and fly to Vegas for the weekend.

The hours in Vegas were a little strange because I lived a nocturnal existence. My shows were at eight o'clock and midnight, and our family dinners were sometimes at ten o'clock, which the kids loved, mostly because it was late. After sleeping late, we would spend time together during the day. When I played the Sands, the hotel would put me up in a three-bedroom suite with a private pool. We even went to church on Saturday evening.

Once when I was playing the Riviera and Bernadette Peters was my opening act, my daughter Courtney made friends with Steve Martin, who was going out with Bernadette at the time. Courtney was six months old, and she was in her baby crib in my dressing room. When Bernadette took the stage, Steve would stop by my dressing room. Steve's routine was the same every time: He would walk in, say hello to Ginnie and me, and then he would stand over Courtney's crib and watch her. He didn't make faces or gestures. He just watched her. Five minutes later, he would tell me to have a good show and leave.

Vegas was never a kids' town, but there were places to amuse the children, like the bumper-car park frequented by the local kids of the cocktail waitresses and blackjack dealers. A hairdresser once told me a story about living in Vegas. She was doing a woman's hair, and her client offhandedly asked her if she flew in and flew out every day. No, the hairdresser explained, she actually lived in Vegas. The woman couldn't grasp the concept that someone was raising a family in Vegas.

It did get lonely when the kids left. On Sundays, I would drive them to the airport, and they would fly home with their babysitter, Rhonda. Ginnie would stay until

Monday to prevent me from having that sinking feeling of my entire family heading home and leaving me behind.

Generally I played Vegas six to eight weeks each year. In the summer when the kids were off from school, I would try to book myself at Harrah's in Lake Tahoe. The casino would give us a beautiful, fully staffed house on the lake with a boat. During the day, we'd go on picnics or swim off the pier. Winters were for skiing and sledding for the kids.

I don't know how normal any of this was, but the kids accepted it as our way of life.

In 1970, I had been on the road doing a series of shows. I was playing the Desert Inn, and the opening act was Edie Adams. She told Ginnie about this wonderful place in Washington State that she had just worked called Ocean Shores. Ginnie immediately decided that we should go there because we hadn't spent enough quality family time together. And, like your average, upper-middle-class American family, we should rent a Winnebago and drive.

"A family vacation would be a bonding experience," she said. It would be a chance to be with the kids and get to know each other better. Parents and kids alike would embark on a time of discovery, learning, and togetherness—not to mention bickering and exhaustion.

Back home, I rented a Winnebago and we filled it with our two sons, Rob, six, and Tim, three; our rambunctious Irish setter, Lady; and enough Jif peanut butter to sink a small boat.

This was 1970, very early on in the evolution of recreational vehicles. Driving an RV is completely different from driving a car. You have to drive a Winnebago from the middle, not from the front the way you drive a car. On any long vehicle, the center is behind you, and you have to maneuver accordingly. Hence the ominous sign you often see on large trucks: "Caution: Vehicle Makes Wide Turns."

Being a typical man, I hadn't read the manual. While I was finding the center, I put a few scrapes on the Winnebago, but nothing major. Every time I made a left turn, the contents of the refrigerator spilled onto the floor.

"Bob, you didn't read the manual, did you?" Ginnie would shout.

"No, honey . . . I didn't."

These mishaps dented my confidence a bit and made me tentative. The Winnebago's height clearance was fourteen feet, so whenever I saw signs on the overpass that read fifteen feet, I didn't quite trust them. I'd slow down and listen closely for a scraping noise. But after whizzing under a few at 40 m.p.h., my confidence grew exponentially.

At night, we would camp in a motor-home park. After leveling the Winnebago, I would fill up the water tanks. Ginnie would shower first, followed by our sons. I was always the last to shower, and, without fail, the water always gave out halfway through my shower. I made a mental note as to which half I had washed, so the next day before the water quit I could wash the other half.

To take a break from the campgrounds—and so I could have a hot shower every few days—we occasionally stayed in hotels. We relied on one of those guidebooks, but the book didn't always have the critical details.

Early one evening, we pulled into a hotel with several motor homes in the parking lot. Upon further inspection, I discovered that all the motor homes were carrying elderly couples. I decided we should find another place—or risk being kept up all night by the paramedics.

By 11:00 P.M. the kids were cranky and Ginnie was nagging me to find someplace, anyplace. I pulled into the first motel I saw and went inside to check in. When I asked for two adjoining rooms, the desk clerk shook his head and laughed.

"What's wrong?" I asked. "You don't have connecting rooms?"

"This is Seafair weekend," he told me.

"It's what?"

"Seafair weekend. You won't find a hotel around these parts for fifty miles."

We pressed on and finally found a place that had a vacancy.

The next day we drove to the hotel where we were going to be staying for a few days. It was Polynesian-themed and its entrance had large wood columns with a thatched roof held up by exotic-looking slanted beams.

As I pulled up to the entrance, the driver in front of our Winnebago motioned for me to change lanes. Without thinking, I maneuvered into the other lane. Unfortunately, the overhead clearance was significantly reduced by the slanted beams. I heard this terrible grinding sound, followed by a loud *thump*, and turned around to see our rooftop air conditioner had crashed through the roof and landed in the middle of the living space.

My three-year-old son, Tim, was standing next to the air conditioner, surveying the wreckage. "Bad daddy! Bad daddy!" he chastised.

Luckily, no one was hurt except for my rented Winnebago. I was in a real predicament. I was in rural Washington State on Seafair weekend with an air conditioning unit in the middle of the floor and a gaping hole in the roof, and I needed to drive back to Los Angeles. The only option was to wake up early the next morning and drive thirty miles to Tacoma to have the air conditioner and the roof repaired.

To further complicate the situation, I had an interview scheduled the following morning with a reporter from a local newspaper. Rather than cancel, I had him ride along. It worked out fine. He sat up front next to me in the captain's chair and shouted his questions over the whooshing sound created by the hole in the roof, and I shouted my answers back.

The Winnebago trip from hell was punctuated by the smell of peanut butter. Every day at lunch, the kids asked for peanut butter and jelly sandwiches. By the end of the trip, Ginnie would get sick to her stomach from the smell. She thought it was because she made the same sandwich every day for two weeks. But it turned out there was another passenger aboard: Ginnie was pregnant with our third child, Jennifer, although she didn't know it.

When we arrived back in Los Angeles, I drove Ginnie straight to the doctor in the Winnebago. "You better be pregnant because that's the only way to explain why we've been fighting so much ... and why we're still riding around in this RV."

They say that a man could never have a child because he couldn't endure the pain of childbirth. But there is still plenty for a man to do. When Ginnie went into labor with our firstborn, Rob, it was around six o'clock in the morning. I was fast asleep.

The sound of a suitcase zipping and unzipping woke me, and Ginnie informed me that it was time to go to the hospital. My immediate reaction was to panic, but having read all these books about what to expect when you're expecting, I knew that I had to remain calm.

"Have you been timing the contractions?" I asked.

"They're five minutes apart," she replied.

One of the library of books I read said that meant we were six hours away from birth. I began to calculate: We are forty-five minutes from the hospital. That's another thing you discover: Every self-respecting obstetrician has his office an hour from the hospital and an hour from your home. This is for the father's benefit so he can go crazy, because from the moment his wife gets pregnant, he has constant visions of not making it to the hospital fast enough and having to deliver the baby in the front seat of the car.

Calmly, I told Ginnie to finish packing. Just an FYI: You never use anything in the suitcase. The books tell you to pack a suitcase, but that's just to give the wife something to do while the husband is getting dressed. The minute you arrive at the hospital, they take the suitcase and shove it off in a corner.

Next, I went into the bathroom, shaved, and put Band-Aids on my face. Ginnie was packed, and I was finally ready.

"Aren't you going to call the doctor?" she asked.

"Of course, that's a very good idea," I said. "He should know about it. He should be there, or at least a representative of his."

I went into the den, looked up his phone number, and called him. When he answered, I yelled, *"Baaaaby!"* and then hung up.

We went downstairs and got in the car. Everything was going smoothly on the drive, except for the three cars in front of us that were driving so slowly I thought they were practicing for a parade. About halfway to the hospital, Ginnie checked to see if I had called the doctor.

"Yes, honey, I did," I assured her. "Dr. Miller will be there in about an hour."

"Dr. Miller is my dentist. What the hell did you call my dentist for?"

"Well . . . doctors talk to other doctors. He'll figure out what to do. Besides, if a cab driver can deliver a baby, then I'm sure a dentist can, too."

When we reached the hospital, Ginnie's contractions were three minutes apart. At this point, you think your troubles should pretty much be over because there are doctors and nurses everywhere. *Wishful* thinking. This is where your troubles begin.

The hospital we went to is strange because they have a parking lot where you have to insert a quarter into a small slot to open the gate. They don't operate on the honor system. Apparently, they think you are going to drop off your wife and take off to Acapulco. Let me tell you, it's not the easiest thing to hit that small opening with a quarter when you're doing 20 m.p.h.

Without incident, we reached the admitting office and Ginnie sat down. The person behind the desk asked my name.

"Mr. Newhart."

"All right, Mr. Newkirk, is this your wife?" she asked.

"No, she's a hitchhiker. She was hitchhiking and she looked pregnant so I picked her up and dropped her off here because it's right on my way to work."

"I see. Well, we have to have the husband here to sign the papers."

"I *am* the husband," I interjected. "That was just a little attempt at humor."

She wasn't amused. "Okay, Mr. Newkirk," she said slowly. "Do you have Blue Cross or any other insurance plan?"

I was growing more antsy by the moment knowing Ginnie's contractions were coming faster. "Could I possibly answer the questions *after* you take my wife upstairs?"

"No, I'm afraid not," she said. "We need your wife to sign the admission form after you answer all of the necessary questions."

"Well, if you wait about fifteen minutes, all three of us can sign the form."

Upon hearing this, she panicked. As it turned out, she was a desk clerk and not a nurse and therefore would not have known what to do if the baby popped out in the lobby. She helped Ginnie into the elevator, and we headed upstairs to the delivery rooms.

They had two wonderfully titled rooms. One was called the "labor room" and the other one was the "hard-labor room," where presumably the woman giving birth could scream her head off. Ginnie chose the hard-labor room, and I was told to wait.

If you are an expectant father, finding out any information from hospital personnel is next to impossible. The expectant father is the lowest form of life. Even maintenance workers will have nothing to do with you. There are people running around with various pans of one kind or another and worried looks on their faces. I'm not even sure they are nurses. They're just people hired to run around looking worried because this makes the expectant father feel like everything is under control.

These days, the father stands at the mother's side and feeds her ice chips. Back then in the sixties, fathers waited in the fathers' room. It's sort of a torture chamber they devised to drive the fathers nuts while their wives are having the babies. There was one guy in there whose wife had already given birth so he was superior to everyone else. He was chewing on a cigar and gloating. I decided to try to get some information out of him.

"They just took my wife in to the hard-labor room," I mentioned. "What'll it be, fifteen, twenty minutes?"

"Oh, no, no, no," he said, shaking his head. "More like five, six, maybe even seven hours. You see that poor guy over there who is humming and not making any sense? Thirty-two hours he's been here."

Thankfully, everything went smoothly. I had only been waiting four hours when the nurse walked in and gave me the good news.

"It's a boy," she said. "Congratulations, Mr. Newkirk."

•

Marriage and fatherhood heighten the disillusion that we all think we are born handy. We confidently believe that we can fix things around the house, as if it's part of the collective male brain that was further enhanced by eighth-grade shop class.

Well, it's not, and being pig-headed about it can become expensive.

One Saturday morning over breakfast, Ginnie instructed me to call a carpenter because we needed to replace a swinging door leading from the garage out to the back-yard area.

"I can do that," I assured her.

"Do you know how to hang a door?" she asked.

"It's a door," I said, brushing her off. "What's so hard about hanging a door?"

I was sure that I was equal to the task because I had once had a summer job in a woodworking plant. The company made faux-cedar chests. They would take a chest made of pine or another cheap wood and then wrap it in sheets of glue and press thin layers of cedar on the chest. It turned out, I was a superstar at this.

On my first day on the job, one of the foremen assigned me to the glue machine.

"Let's take a standard order, which is ten twelve-inch pieces of glue," he said. "I'm going to take this chalk and then I am going to mark twelve inches. I am going to roll out the glue until it reaches twelve inches, and then I am going to use this little razor on top to cut it." He paused to allow all of this to sink in. "How many more pieces of glue would we need to fill this order?"

"Nine," I said.

"Have you worked this machine before?"

I assured him that I hadn't.

"All right," he said. "Let me give you another one. This is eight inches. What are we going to do with the chalk?"

"Put a mark at eight inches."

"Okay, the order calls for nine glue sheets. You've done the one. How many more are you going to do?"

"Eight."

"You've worked this machine before, haven't you?" he asked in amazement.

Notwithstanding my apprenticeship in the mock-cedar-chest business, it turns out that hanging a door is one of the most difficult things you can do.

I drove to the hardware store to buy the supplies. I began to feel a tad intimidated just waiting to be helped. Standing in line with me were professional workmen. You can spot these guys instantly because their hands are covered in bandages from cutting themselves up, and their arms are scraped from falling off a roof or two. When it was my turn, I asked the salesman for a door.

"You want a hollow door or a solid door?" he asked.

"Uh . . . solid door," I said, reasoning that it would be stronger.

By the way, you don't want a solid door for a swinging door. A solid door weighs fifty pounds and a hollow door weighs five pounds, creating the need for two people to hold the door while a third person attaches the hinges.

The salesman scribbled on a piece of paper. "What are you going into?" he asked.

"What?"

"What is the house made of? Cement? Stucco? Wood?"

"It's stucco," I guessed. "And I'm going to need some screws."

"What do you want? Half inch? Three-quarter inch? Inch-and-a-quarter?"

I guessed again. "Inch-and-a-quarter."

"Are you going to shield them?"

"Am I going to shield what?"

"The screws."

"Yeah, of course. I wouldn't put screws into stucco without shielding them."

After buying all the necessary saws, planes, and levels, I headed home with my solid door, inch-and-a-quarter screws, and shields for the screws. I spent the rest of the afternoon hanging the door. When I finished, my back ached. My arms felt like soggy noodles. And the door had a gaping space at the bottom from where I had sawed too much off.

The following day I called a carpenter. By this point, I was in for three times the cost, with a garage full of tools and an unusable door.

When we moved into our second house, I called in the pros. This, however, comes with a whole different set of problems. For starters, you have to speak their language or you can't get anything done. Contractors have a particularly complicated jargon.

We wanted to install a fireplace in our den, so I pointed to a corner where I thought it would fit nicely.

"That's a bearing wall, you know," the contractor said.

"Oh, yeah, I forgot. We can't have a fireplace on a bearing wall." I nodded. "Maybe we could warm up the feeling of the room by putting in some lights and crown molding."

"Nope, you'll be going into a soffit."

Years later, I did complete one house project that I was proud of because it utilized my skills as a comedian. I noticed that all the houses in the neighborhood had signs to ward off prowlers: "Caution: Attack Dog" or "Armed Guard on Duty." I drove down to the hardware store and ordered a warning sign that read "Armed Dog."

People were so conditioned to the other signs, no one ever said a word about mine.

CHAPTER EIGHT

They Should've Pulled
My Psychologist's License

My father did finally notice me when I became successful. Around 1978, *The Bob Newhart Show* went into syndication. My sisters used to tell me that my dad would call around to the local stations and ask them why they weren't running his son's show. When I returned to Chicago to shoot a commercial promoting the show, I arranged for him to be in the spot with me. That's what it took to get his attention, but that's not why I did the show.

By the time I had my third child, I was somewhat financially stable, but I was also traveling more than I liked. As the kids grew older, it was hard for them to travel because of school, friends, and activities. Sitting alone in hotel room after hotel room, I often thought about cutting down on my days on the road.

The salvation came in 1971 when my manager, Arthur Price, asked me if I would like to do a TV show. Absolutely, I told him. A TV series would be steady work, and it would get me off the road and allow me to be home nights and weekends like nine-to-five working parents.

After leaving the talent management firm Bernard, Williams and Price, Artie cofounded the TV production company MTM Enterprises with Mary Tyler Moore and her husband, Grant Tinker. He also continued to manage Mary and me. At the time, MTM had the hot hand in town in TV with *The Mary Tyler Moore Show*, and CBS wanted another show from MTM.

That's how it works in the TV business. If you produce a hit show, the network will buy your next idea. Even if it's two guys standing across a room from each other, throwing a ball back and forth, the network will order thirteen episodes without blinking.

So Artie pulled two writers, David Davis and Lorenzo Music, off *The Mary Tyler Moore Show* to create a show for me.

The first idea Davis and Music had was for me to play a psychiatrist. They knew my telephone comedy routines well. In fact, Music had cowritten an air-traffic-controller skit that I performed on *The Smothers Brothers Comedy Hour*. As Davis put it, I listened funny. So in searching for a profession to take advantage of me being a reactor to various situations, they floated the idea of psychiatry.

I resisted. I didn't like the idea of being a psychiatrist because they deal with seriously ill people. I didn't want to be doing a show about a doctor treating a patient with multiple personalities or bipolar disorder. "As much as that appeals to me, that shouldn't be where we get our humor," I explained.

I suggested making the character a psychologist because they deal with less seriously disturbed people. A psychologist would be seeing a guy who won't get on the plane, while a psychiatrist would be treating a guy who wants to blow it up because he doesn't like the Salisbury steak. So my newest job was as a psychologist, "a serious albeit unspectacular profession," according to Dr. Robert Hartley himself.

We honestly weren't sure how the audience would react to a psychologist as an occupation. Most people think psychologists are nuttier than the people they treat. In college, all the psych majors were off by themselves in the corner of the library, reading obscure books, fidgeting with their horn-rimmed glasses, and carrying on conversations with themselves.

Originally we also made my office suite-mate, played by Peter Bonerz, a psychologist. For contrast, Peter was going to be a radical psychologist who was into wild treatments like primal screaming. But this proved to be too much, so the character was changed to a children's orthodontist.

In the fourth season, we did an episode that addressed the skepticism toward psychologists. It's one of the episodes most often mentioned to me by people who remember the show. A seemingly friendly talk-show hostess named Ruth Corley invites Dr. Hartley on her morning show. He arrives expecting a softball interview, but he ends up being excoriated.

His rude awakening begins with Corley's introduction: "It's been said that today's psychologist is nothing more than a con man, a snake-oil salesman flimflamming innocent people, peddling cures for everything from nail biting to a lousy love life—and I agree. We'll ask Dr. Hartley to defend himself after these messages."

Later in the interview, she calls Bob on the carpet about whether or not he cures his patients.

"You mean you ask forty dollars an hour and you guarantee nothing?" she says.

"Well, I validate."

"Is that your answer? Do you ever cure anybody?"

"Well . . . I wouldn't say 'cure.' "

"So your answer is no."

"No, my answer is not no. . . . I get results."

As Bob leaves, he passes two nuns on their way to being interviewed and quips: "I'll go fifty-fifty on a hit man."

But even the most casual viewer of the show knows that Dr. Hartley's regular patients were no better off on their last visit to Room 715 on the seventh floor of the Timpau Medical Arts Building than they were on their first.

Mr. Peterson remains meek and scared of everything from his wife, to upholstery, to geese. Mrs. Bakerman, who describes herself as a "weirdette," has no obvious hang-ups, and therefore none are cured. Michele Nardo continues to have trouble getting a date and is afraid to be seen in a swimsuit. And Mr. Carlin, his premiere patient, continues to harbor hostility and insensitivity to others' feelings.

A typical session is one during which Mr. Carlin informs Dr. Hartley of his progress. "I think I'm overcoming my agoraphobia," Mr. Carlin says.

"I didn't even know you had a fear of open places," Bob says.

"Open places?"

"Agoraphobia is a fear of open places."

"I thought it was a fear of agricultural products."

"Sorry . . ."

"Well, anyway, wheat doesn't scare me anymore. I'm still a little skittish around barley."

Another day, Mr. Carlin appears and announces, "I only had one problem this week. Yesterday, I was possessed by the devil." To which Dr. Hartley says, "Okay, go with that, Mr. Carlin."

Here's a classic phone conversation with a "cured" patient: "Mrs. Harlick, we've been over this before," Dr. Hartley says. "As you said yourself, you overeat because having a beautiful body threatens you, and for some reason, having a fat body doesn't threaten you. . . . I'm happy to hear you've been able to control it. Mrs. Harlick, I can't understand you with your mouth full."

Some, like the ventriloquist's dummy who wants to break up the act and go out on his own, were probably incurable from the start.

But for all the uncured patients, Dr. Hartley did do some good. A woman once wrote me a letter saying that she and her husband were having problems with their son and so they told the boy they wanted him to try therapy. They asked if he would mind getting some professional help to straighten out his problems. The boy asked his parents if the doctor would be like that man on television. When the parents assured them he was, the boy agreed to go.

•

The question of Bob Hartley's TV wife and kids came up early in the discussions with Davis and Music. Finding a wife proved to be almost as difficult as it was in real life. We read several very good actresses, but no one really clicked with me.

Then one morning, Artie called. "I think I've found your wife," he said.

"Oh, I didn't know she was missing," I replied.

Budumbump. He explained that he was watching *The Tonight Show* the previous evening and Suzanne Pleshette was Johnny's guest. "She'd be great," he said. "She's her own woman. It will be an ideal marriage."

I agreed. I knew Suzie socially, but I questioned whether or not she would do television. She had acted in several feature films, including *If It's Tuesday, This Must Be Belgium; The Birds;* and *Nevada Smith.* She had also appeared on Broadway in *The Miracle Worker.* Though she had starred in some TV movies, hers wasn't a name that would have been on the casting list for a sitcom.

Artie called her agent, and it turned out she was interested. Because Suzie had spent most of her career working on location, she, too, wanted to get off the road and have more of a normal kind of life.

Suzie hadn't done situation comedy, but she dove into the process. While taping one of the first episodes, she pulled me aside and asked why she was saying a line about a lawyer. I explained to her that the line was a playback on an earlier lawyer line. From then on, every time we had a similar situation she'd say, "This is a lawyer joke again, right?"

On camera, we clicked. The chemistry was perfect. Bob and Emily were a modernized couple for the seventies, and there was the perfect amount of tension, love, and respect to make the marriage feel real. They also got on each other's nerves the way spouses do.

In one episode, Bob is in bed eating a bowl of cereal annoyingly.

Emily: "Do you know that you always chew your food thirty-two times?"

Bob: "Yeah, my mother taught me that. She used to say thirty-two times keeps your tummy from danger, then you can stay up and listen to *The Lone Ranger*."

Emily: "Stop it. It's been driving me up the wall for six years."

Somewhat radical for the time, they were shown sleeping in the same bed. We were one of the first shows to suggest that Bob and Emily had a sex life—quite something for a TV sitcom in 1972.

At the end of the first episode, in which Emily is scared to fly to New York with Bob and a group of patients, Bob receives a phone message from his wife saying that he was sensational. Jerry, Bob's suite-mate, overhears this and queries Bob.

Jerry: "I didn't think Emily went to New York with you."

Bob: "No, she didn't. She was referring to something that happened this morning."

Years later, when I did the sitcom *Newhart* and Mary Frann was cast as my wife, I told Mary that she had one of the hardest jobs in TV because everyone was going to compare her to Suzanne. It didn't help that I once called her "Emily" in the middle of a taping. All in all, I think Mary did a great job carrying the burden and creating her own, unique on-camera relationship with me.

As to the issue of Bob and Emily Hartley having kids, the only other real creative demand I had was that I didn't want them to have children. I didn't want to be the dolt of a father who gets himself in trouble and then the precocious kids huddle in the kitchen and plot a way to get Dad out of this pickle.

My own kids didn't seem to mind that they had no namesakes on TV. They were just happy with all the new toys.

The producers, however, had agreed that if Suzie became pregnant in real life during filming we would make Emily pregnant. Though that never happened, in the fifth year of the show, the producers hatched an idea for Emily to get pregnant. They commissioned a script and sent it over to me.

The next day, one of the producers called me and asked what I thought.

"It's a very funny script," I said.

"Oh, I'm glad you like it," the producer said. "We were really nervous about your reaction."

"I only have one question," I said. "Who are you going to get to play the part of Bob?"

•

If I had to place a number on it, I would say that Bob Hartley was 85 percent me, 15 percent TV character.

Bob Hartley was not in the mold of Ozzie Nelson of *Ozzie and Harriet* or Robert Young's Jim Anderson from *Father Knows Best*. He had flaws, though not as many as *All in the Family*'s Archie Bunker. While he was amiable, well-intentioned, and generally easygoing, he could also be petulant, peevish, and egotistical.

As I said, 85 percent real Bob, 15 percent TV Bob.

He also had an everyman quality. Every wife who

watched would come away saying, "that's exactly what my husband would do," and every guy would say, "I almost did the same thing." You are dealing with human nature, which truly doesn't change that much, so it's easy to find the truth.

When Bob finds out that Emily's IQ is higher than his, all of his flaws surface. In the episode, Emily, who is a part-time teacher, is assigned to administer IQ tests. She first tries to give a practice test to their loopy neighbor Howard, who quips, "I hope the test isn't as hard as the directions." And then she convinces Bob to take the test.

The following day, Emily grades the test. Bob can't wait to find out his score.

"Emily, if I can give up three hours of my life to take the IQ test, you can give up three seconds of your life to answer it for me," Bob tells her. "What was the score?"

"I don't think people should know their IQs," she says.

"Well, you know your IQ."

"That's different. I have to know mine."

"I have to know mine. What was it?"

"One hundred and twenty-nine."

"One hundred and twenty-nine . . . that's good, isn't it?"

"That's very good, Bob," she says with sincere flattery. "That's almost gifted."

"Almost gifted. . . . What's yours?"

"It's not important."

"I know it's not important, but what is it?"

Emily laughs girlishly. "I'm embarrassed."

"Well, honey, don't be embarrassed. I had four more years of college than you. I have a Ph.D."

"Bob, it's one hundred and fifty-one."

"That's good, too."

Of course Bob can't let go of this. A little later in the episode, he tells Emily that her higher IQ is affecting their marriage, but she tries to downplay the situation.

"What's it got to do with us?" she says. "We've got a perfect marriage."

"Emily, a perfect marriage is where a husband and a wife have the same IQ."

"Bob, it's not important. . . ."

"Next to perfect is where the husband's is higher than the wife's. . . ."

"Bob, forget it."

"Third is where the husband's is one point higher than the wife's . . ."

"Bob, please forget it."

"Fourth, which is us, which is the worst, is where the wife is one hundred and fifty-one and the husband is one hundred and twenty-nine, which is difference of . . . of . . ."

"Twenty-two."

Petulant, peevish, and a little egotistical. By the way, if you are a guy I wouldn't bother to find out your IQ. Based on my experience, your wife probably does have a higher IQ than you.

•

It was my idea to set *The Bob Newhart Show* in Chicago. Besides the fact that I was associated with Chicago, the other big cities were taken. *The Jeffersons* was set in New York. Even Minneapolis was taken by *The Mary Tyler Moore Show*.

The setting was really more a state of mind because we didn't shoot on location in Chicago. The shows were filmed in Hollywood before a live television audience. Only the opening title sequence was filmed in Chicago—with an unintentional air of corruption, I might add.

Are you familiar with the signature image of Dr. Bob Hartley walking across the Chicago River in the opening titles?

Well, it's not me.

On the particular day we shot that sequence, my daughter Jennifer came down with roseola, so Ginnie and I spent the day in the hospital with her. The show only had the location for one day, so the producers hired an actor to study my walk and stroll across the bridge. To this day, I have no idea who he is.

There's another problem in the opening credits. Every day, I miss my stop. Bob Hartley takes the Ravenswood line of the "L" (as the elevated train is known) to Glencoe—and then walks back fifty-five blocks to Belmont and Sheridan, the station stop for his apartment. Now, would you trust a man who missed his stop by fifty-five blocks every day?

While we're at it, Bob and Emily live on the fifth floor of the ten-story Meridian Beach apartment building on Lake Shore Drive. The apartment shown in the exterior shots is clearly on the seventh floor of a sixteen-story building, which, in reality, is Buckingham Plaza, located at the corner of East Randolph Street and Lake Shore Drive. That's the magic of TV.

Every now and then there were inaccuracies that needed to be corrected by a Chicago native. One scene called for me to attend a Cubs game at night at a time when there were no lights at Wrigley Field.

Apparently, *The Bob Newhart Show* did have something of a positive impact on the city. At the entrance to the Navy Pier, now the most popular family destination in Chicago, sits a statue of me as Dr. Bob Hartley.

The statue has Dr. Hartley sitting in his chair, facing a two-seat couch, where passersby can sit and discuss their problems. It's one in a series placed around the country by TV Land, along with Mary Tyler Moore in Minneapolis; Andy Griffith in Mt. Airy, North Carolina; and Jackie Gleason in a New York City bus terminal.

Seeing it for the first time was surreal. Originally it was located on Michigan Avenue near the Western Federal Bank building—a spot I used to walk past every day in college. If someone had told me then that there was going to be a statue of me in downtown Chicago, I would have asked for a hit of whatever he was smoking.

Nevertheless, I've always wondered why the statue is three-quarter size. That would never have happened had the show been set in New York.

•

I never really understood why *The Bob Newhart Show* never won any Emmys. The show was nominated fifteen times in various categories over eight years, and we didn't win a single one.

In my mind, the strike against us was that our cast was a true ensemble—Suzanne, Bill Daily, Marcia Wallace, Tom Poston, Peter Bonerz. These actors were so damn good, and they made it look so easy, that they weren't recognized. To this day, that frustrates me. If you have to hit marks and speak other people's words, that's not merely being yourself; it's acting.

We also didn't do shows on the heady material that Emmy voters seem to prefer. Our idea of a serious issue was when Emily and I were having a costume party at our apartment and Jerry arrives wearing an Uncle Sam costume. Then Marsha comes in wearing an Uncle Sam costume. Finally, Howard enters in the same Uncle Sam costume.

"That's weird," Jerry says. "We all rented the same costume."

Howard replies, "What do you mean 'rented'?"

That should've been worthy of at least a best teleplay Emmy right there.

•

After five seasons, *The Bob Newhart Show* was still at the top of its game, which is exactly where I wanted to end it. The problem was that CBS had me under contract for another year. I decided to personally ask Bob Daly and Robert Wussler, who were coheads of CBS entertainment, to let me out of my contract.

I met with Daly and Wussler in a bungalow at the Beverly Hills Hotel. Daly told me that they really wanted me to come back for a sixth season. I didn't have much chance to plead my case because ringing phones constantly interrupted the meeting with an even bigger crisis.

That afternoon, in a heavily promoted CBS special presentation, Evel Knievel was scheduled to jump over several motorhomes on his bike. Telly Savalas was hosting the event. Unfortunately, Evel had taken a nasty spill during a practice run so there wasn't going to be any death-defying jump. Daly instructed New York to have Telly keep talking until they figured out what to do.

A few days later, my attorney clarified CBS's position. "Bob, if you don't do a sixth year and they put another show in your time slot that doesn't do as well, they would have a right to sue you for the difference between what your show would've generated in revenue and what the replacement show generates," he explained.

"Downside, how much are we talking about here?" I asked.

"About fifty or sixty million dollars . . ."

So I returned for the sixth season.

> ❯ ❯ ❯ ❯ ❯

CHAPTER NINE

The Lubitsch Touch:
My Days on the Big Screen

In September of 1960 my agents at MCA arranged a meeting with filmmaker Bob Pirosh about his World War II
movie titled *Hell Is for Heroes*. Naturally, I assumed it was
because the director had done his homework and learned
about my military experience of serving as a personnel
specialist who could not be sent overseas and was, in retro-
spect, the final line of defense for the homeland.

In any event, at the time of the meeting with Pirosh,
my album *The Button-Down Mind of Bob Newhart* was
No. 1 on the record album charts. Given Pirosh's varied
resume—director of *Valley of the Kings*, an action movie
about the search for an ancient Egyptian tomb, and writer
of several episodes of the TV shows *Bonanza* and *My
Three Sons*—there was really no way to know where all of
this was going. So it was under these circumstances that I
met with Pirosh in New York at the Hampshire House,
where I was staying.

Pirosh outlined his screenplay for *Hell Is for Heroes*. I

suppose you would call it a lighthearted look at World War II, or at least that's how it started out. Based on what I think was an actual event, the story is about a division that is pulled off the Siegfried Line in Montigny, France. All that's left behind is a squad of men whose job it is to deceive the Germans into believing that they are the great Allied Task Force until reinforcements arrive.

They wanted me for the part of Pfc. James E. Driscoll, a clerk-typist with no combat experience. Driscoll winds up in this particular unit when he gets lost driving a shipment of typewriters to headquarters. The undermanned squad commandeers him and his jeep. Because Driscoll can't handle a weapon and the Germans are monitoring the Americans' phone lines, he is ordered to ad lib phony phone conversations to create the illusion that troop levels are high and morale is strong. My role would be to write one-sided telephone routines similar to those in my popular stand-up act and perform them in the movie.

In short, Pirosh believed that a war movie is hell without some humor in it, and that was where I came in.

The trick of these routines was to have the jokes quietly sneak up on the audience, while also making them credible enough to throw off the eavesdropping German soldiers. In the first bit I did in the movie, I began by promoting my character and then went into a ruse about our unit's most serious problems. *"This is Lt. Driscoll, the entertainment officer....About the morale, sir. It's been rather low. The main complaint seems to be about the evening movie.... Yes, sir.... I've had to show* Road to Morocco *five evenings in a row, sir. Well, the men are beginning to get a little surly, sir.... Yes, sir, they know all the lines.... Oh, the amateur hours are going very well, sir. Sir, could you hold on just a minute...? Yes, sir, I have a call on the other line.... Right, sir. I'll be right back.* (I answer the fake call.) *This is Lt. Driscoll.... Don't, don't send 'em up here! Sir, I have five men in each foxhole now. I don't have any room for any more, sir. Have you tried Charlie Company?... Oh, I see. Well, sir, there's been a war going on in Japan. You might send them over there."*

I kicked off the second by letting the audience in on the joke and kept up with the "sirs." *"Major Winston's jeep— right, sir. We'll certainly be on the lookout for it, sir.... A private, first class, you say... with a load of typewriters in the back. If we see him, we'll contact you, sir.... Blanke the cook is working out rather well, sir.... Well, one problem is that his vichyssoise tastes a little too much like potato soup.... Oh, it's supposed to taste like potato soup."*

Blanke was actually Henry Blanke, the film's producer, and from what I had heard, a case study in persistence. Back in the 1930s, Warner Bros. had given Blanke a generous contract as a producer to duplicate what the studios called "The Lubitsch Touch," which, by the way, is a great film school phrase.

Named for Ernst Lubitsch, director of such films as *Heaven Can Wait* and *The Shop Around the Corner,* this ethereal quality gives a film a feeling of sophistication and leaves the audience feeling worldly. Studios were so eager to re-create The Lubitsch Touch that they were hiring anyone who had any association with Lubitsch. Blanke's connection was that he had come to the United States from Germany as part of Lubitsch's original crew. Never mind that he was his assistant. That was close enough for the studios.

Blanke had a nice run as a producer. He worked as a production supervisor under the legendary producer Hal B. Wallis, and his films collected nine Oscar nominations for best picture, with one win for *The Life of Emile Zola*. But by the late 1950s, Blanke was losing his Lubitsch Touch, and Warner Bros. was looking for a way of getting out of his contract. The studio lawyers studied the contract and concluded it didn't actually specify that Blanke be employed as a producer. As long as he was paid $2,500 a week, the obligation was fulfilled. So in an effort to embarrass Blanke into leaving, the brothers Warner informed him that henceforth he would be in charge of the shoeshine stand.

Blanke, however, was unfazed. The following morning, he dutifully showed up with a full regalia of shoeshine equipment—polish, brushes, and spit-shining cloths. Eventually he was loaned out to Paramount, where his first film was *Hell Is for Heroes*. It was also his last film ever.

•

Between my meeting with Bob Pirosh in the fall of 1960 and the start of filming in July 1961, the movie took on a different shape. Pirosh was replaced as director by Don Siegel, who later went on to do several Clint Eastwood films, including *Dirty Harry*. The two directors were opposites. Where Pirosh saw the more comedic aspects of war, Siegel was focused on its futility. Pirosh's version was budgeted for ten explosions; Siegel ended up with 10,000. In Pirosh's version, James Coburn had a pet duck. The only duck on Siegel's set would be served at lunch, Peking style.

The cast was filled with a gallery of lovable rogues: Bobby Darin, Fess Parker, Harry Guardino, Nick Adams, and the relatively unknown Coburn. But to the chagrin of Darin, who was apparently under the impression that his name would be atop the marquee, a true rogue was added to the cast: Steve McQueen.

As the poster, which now hangs in my garage, declared: "The most exciting young stars of our time hit it big in the hit for all ages."

The plot was rejiggered around McQueen's rebel image, and it became a story about a solitary hero bucking the system and ordering an unauthorized attack on a Nazi pillbox. McQueen sharpened his method-acting skills to play the part. Before filming, he met with the cast and told us in his trademark low-key fashion how things would go during filming. "Man, I like you guys," he said. "But, man, I'm not supposed to like you in the movie, man, so I've got to live apart from you guys and not have anything to do with you guys during the shoot." We all told McQueen that was fine with us, man.

Things did not go smoothly once filming began. For weeks on end, we climbed up hills and ran back down them. The temperature reached 117 degrees in the shade, only there was no shade. Day sequences were changed to night so the actors wouldn't expire in the heat. In one scene where the stoic McQueen was supposed to cry, he couldn't muster a single tear. Siegel tried everything. He slapped McQueen in the face before one take and ran away, but that only made McQueen mad. A fan was rigged to blow onions in McQueen's face, but it was no use.

During the shoot, McQueen and Darin grew increas-

ingly cranky over who the star really was, and stories began winding up in the Hollywood trade papers about them
feuding on the set. The unit publicist was fingered for the
leaks and was summarily dismissed. Unfortunately, they
had the wrong man. It turned out that Nick Adams was
trading with the gossipmongers: some dirt from the set in
exchange for a splashy item on his next movie. But upon
hearing the unit publicist had been fired, Adams felt terribly guilty. I'll never forget the image of Adams chasing
the guy's plane down the runway, yelling out: "I'm sorry.
I'm sorry!"

My career had taken on a different shape, too. *The
Button-Down Mind of Bob Newhart* was well on its way to
selling more than a million copies, and *The Button-Down
Mind Strikes Back* was also climbing the record album
charts. My money for performing in nightclubs had qua-
drupled, and I wanted to accept some of the offers that
were coming my way. Problem was, I was locked in to performing in the movie for a fixed number of weeks.

It was something of a dilemma. I found myself committed to a movie that was totally different than the one I
agreed to, but that alone wasn't a legitimate out for a
rookie actor. There was no clause in my contract stating
that I would be allowed to approve any changes, and I
didn't dare protest too hard for fear of Blanke assigning
me to shoeshine duty. So I concluded that the only grace-
ful exit was to find a way of getting killed.

On a daily basis, I would pester Don Siegel with sugges-
tions for my premature demise. I was aiming for just the
right amount of verisimilitude.

"Now, Don, in this particular scene I see that a tank is

coming over the hill," I said one day. "Maybe—and I'm just offering this up because it could be funny—but maybe I could roll under the tank and get killed."

Siegel's reply: "Bob, you're on the movie until the end."

Frankly I didn't see why he needed me. It seemed to me that once I had delivered my one-sided telephone conversations, I could be eliminated at any point without hurting the movie. He had actors like Steve McQueen, Fess Parker, and Jim Coburn, who were much more convincing in battle scenes than me. Far more important members of the squad had been killed, like Harry Guardino. My gosh, Guardino had been in *King of Kings* as Barabbas, the notorious robber whom Pontius Pilate proposed to condemn to death instead of Jesus, and he had costarred in *Houseboat* alongside Cary Grant and Sophia Loren. Surely if Siegel didn't need Guardino until the last frame of the film, then he didn't need Newhart.

Taking a different tack, I tried again. Early in the movie, when Driscoll picks up a rifle for the first time, he accidentally pulls the trigger and nearly shoots one of his fellow squad members. After being taught how to point and shoot, Driscoll is nicknamed "dead eye" for his inability to hit the intended target. In keeping with the film's integrity, I came up with an idea.

"Perhaps," I proposed to Siegel, "it's late at night . . . The squad is advancing . . . A firefight ensues . . . and Driscoll accidentally puts a slug in someone's rear. Then the guy, thinking that a Nazi has shot him, turns around and shoots Driscoll dead."

This was met with an icy stare and a "you're in the movie until the end."

"How about an unfortunate land-mine accident? A faulty grenade? Electrocution from the radio wire . . . Sir?"

"Newhart, you're in 'till the end," Siegel emphasized.

Fortunately for me, though not for Siegel, the end came sooner than any of us expected. I later read that Blanke had a saying: "You should think of each shot as you make it as the most important one in the film." That couldn't have been closer to the truth than on *Hell Is for Heroes*. In an effort to contain the film, whose budget had climbed from $900,000 to $1,900,000, Paramount stopped sending raw film stock to the set. The studio brass laid down the law: When the film stock ran out, the movie was over.

It shows in the finished film. In the final scene, Mc-Queen blows up the German pillbox and himself, and the movie ends on this mundane note. No further explanation is given. Perhaps therein lies the genius of the movie. In later years, *Hell Is for Heroes* developed a cult following. It has been shown on TV far more than other more accomplished war movies with tidy conclusions. I guess audiences like the incomplete ending because it allows them to make up what they believe happened. I'll tell you what happened to Driscoll: The day the film stock ran out, he got on a real life phone and had a two-sided conversation with his agent and booked some lucrative club dates.

•

Apparently I was so good in my first military comedy that Mike Nichols cast me as the character Major Major in his big-screen version of *Catch-22*. Though I felt a little like I was becoming the John Wayne of comedians, I was honored that Mike wanted to work with me. After all, he had just made *The Graduate*.

Catch-22 turned out better than *Hell Is for Heroes*, but its thunder was stolen by Robert Altman's *MASH*, which came out first. Looking back, this is one of those movies where they should have released *The Making of Catch-22*.

A great amount of detail went into the movie. In particular, I remember the wardrobe guy coming up to me and telling me they wore two kinds of shoes. "Today, I am going to have you wear these," he said, holding up a brown pair. "But they also wore these," he added, holding up a less brown pair.

That day I was filming an important scene. Major Major was pacing in his office, giving a speech. There was a picture on the wall behind me, and each time I passed by it would change. The first time I walked by it was Stalin. When I crossed back, it had changed to Roosevelt. More pacing and it became Churchill. The rotating picture was meant to enhance the surreal aspect of the movie.

The scene was filmed as one long, master shot with no close-ups. After the first take, Mike asked (as he always did) if I was happy with it. "Yes," I told him. Then Mike said (as he always did after any actor told him they were pleased), "Let's just do one where you do whatever you want." I said (as I always did), "That's kind of what I wanted." Mike was fine, so we moved on.

As I walked away from the set, I saw the wardrobe guy walking over to me. I excepted him to say something like, "I've been in the movie business thirty-five years. I've worked with Gable and Lombard, and that is the single funniest scene I have ever seen." Instead, he said to me, "Did Mike say anything about the shoes?" To him, it was a scene about shoes.

Catch-22 was set in Sardinia, Italy. However, most of it was shot in Guaymas, Mexico, which doesn't look a lot like Sardinia. They did do some filming in Rome, but I wasn't involved in that part.

The scheduling wasn't all that precise. Undoubtedly, the schedule wasn't helped by the flying sequences. The crew would line up these authentic B-26s, and they'd all take off and fly in formation. If Mike didn't like the shot, he'd cut the scene. The crew would radio the pilots, and the planes would circle, land, and start over again. It took half a day to reset the planes.

In any event, at one point during filming, Norm Fell, who played my aide, and I ended up with ten days off. We decided to take our furlough back home in Los Angeles.

The cast was staying in a hotel called the Playa de Cortez, and my room had a nice view of the sea. I didn't want to lose it, so I decided to keep my room during my break from filming. Norm planned to check out, but he had some laundry coming back and asked to put it in my room. I told him that was fine so he flagged down the maid.

"Señor and myself are flying to Los Angeles," he said slowly to the maid while making a flying gesture with his hand. "I have some laundry"—he grabbed his shirt— "coming back, but I'm giving up my room." He rapidly opened and closed the door and pointed into my room. "But señor"—he pointed to me—"is keeping his room, so when my laundry"—again, he grabbed his shirt—"comes back, would you put it in his room?"

The maid looked at him and, in perfect English, said, "When your laundry comes back, you want me to put it in his room."

After our ten-day break, Norm and I flew back to Hermosillo through Tucson. We were flying with Martin Balsam, who had just been hired to play Col. Cathcart.

The colonel had been a hard part to cast. George C. Scott had supposedly turned down the role because he felt it was too close to the character he played in *Dr. Strangelove.* Stacy Keach was hired and then fired by Mike Nichols. No one quite knew why, but a shiver went through the cast. Each day, we'd wonder, "Did Mike seem funny toward me today or was it just my imagination?"

Making small talk with Marty, I asked him if he had read the script.

"I'm halfway through it," he said, which nicely summed up the entire movie.

On the flight, Norm and I were wondering if anything had happened while we were gone. The atmosphere on location was so surreal that nothing ever seemed to happen. I told Norm that I was sure we'd hear right away of any firings, misdeeds, or other assorted chaos.

When we arrived on the set, we both asked around for news. One crew member told us that it rained one day, forcing them to shoot inside. That was about it, and we thought nothing of the lack of stories. It was the kind of place where no news is no news.

Two weeks later, a group of us were standing around waiting to be called to the set. Jack Gilford announced that he was going into town that afternoon and asked if anyone wanted him to pick up any sundries. Tony Perkins off-handedly volunteered to go with Jack.

"I haven't been in Guaymas since the elephant's funeral," Tony said.

I stopped him right there. "I know that elephants are not indigenous to Mexico because I've read a lot," I said. "What are you talking about?"

"Oh, that's right," Tony said very plainly. "You guys were away. The circus was coming through town, and they had a flatbed truck with an elephant chained to it. The truck went around a curve too fast, the elephant leaned off the edge, and a Greyhound bus hit him and killed him."

Tony shook his head in sadness. "They had a funeral for the elephant. There was nothing to do so everybody attended the funeral."

•

Leaving *Catch-22* was almost as difficult as getting off of *Hell Is for Heroes*. Dick Benjamin, Paula Prentiss, and I were riding in a car to Hermosillo to catch a flight back to Los Angeles. We had been on location for two months straight and couldn't wait to get back to a choice of restaurants, the possibility of an earthquake, and gridlocked traffic.

Suddenly a helicopter buzzed overhead and then started circling low in front of us, clearly indicating that we should pull over. It either meant that Dick or I had to return to the set, or that we were being held up by some very wealthy bandits. Turned out, it was the former.

I should've followed Art Garfunkel's lead. After shooting his scene, Art explained to Mike Nichols that he needed to be back in New York for an important obliga-tion. Probably a concert in Central Park with Paul Simon. He asked Mike for a specific date that he could leave, so he could notify the folks in New York.

Mike explained that he needed to check the film before he could release Art to make sure he had the scene. The film would be sent out that day, but being that it was a Fri-day, the editors wouldn't look at it until Monday. They would develop it on Tuesday and cut it on Wednesday, meaning that it would be flown back on Thursday. This timeline meant that Mike would watch it at the end of the shoot on Friday.

Upon hearing that he was required to hang around for another week, Art returned to the hotel, packed his bags, and called a cab. When the cab arrived, he instructed the driver to take him to the airport in Tucson, which was 200 miles away. Art volunteered to pay the fare both ways. The Mexican cab driver smiled and hit the road for what would be his last fare before retiring in the lap of luxury.

We never saw him again.

•

But serving under Pirosh and Nichols was better than working for Alex Segal, who directed a terrible movie made for television that I starred in with Jill St. John and Jean Simmons called *Decisions! Decisions!* You see, I learned from Johnny that if you are going down, you take everyone with you.

On the first day of shooting, Segal and I were walking and talking about the script. The people who put up the money were Hollywood neophytes who had made their money somewhere else and decided that it would be fun to make a TV movie. They were very nice people, as they always are. "Look who they got as an assistant director," Segal said. "This guy has been after me for a long time."

It wasn't long before I became the target of Segal's paranoia. A couple days after Ginnie and I spent a pleasant evening at his house, we were shooting a scene in which I was in bed wearing a full-body cast. Following Segal's detailed instructions, the prop masters spent an hour putting me in the cast and hoisting me onto the hospital bed.

The moment they finished this process, Segal barked: "Okay, everyone . . . let's take lunch."

•

I don't go through an Actors Studio process of finding a character. In the Actors Studio, they teach what's known as method acting. They instruct you to build a history of your character going back to its childhood. Someone took his rubber ducky away from him in the bathtub when he was five, therefore he's homicidal. Or if you are going to play a garbage collector, you volunteer to ride around with your local waste management crew. If a script is given to me that is humorous, I find where the joke is and I figure out how to get there.

The closest I came to method technique was using the traits of some of my friends from the routines that I created. The submarine commander became the basis for several jobs I held on the big screen because he was the perfect representation of the "Peter Principle" (you rise to your level of incompetence), as well as the ultimate bureaucrat who just wants his one final mission to go right so he can retire.

In the movie *In & Out*, I played a high school principal who was very close to the submarine commander. The principal's entire professional life had been very simple and unexciting. As his name, Tom Halliwell, conveyed, he had been principal for years and all had gone well. He was nearing a smooth and easy retirement, and then all of a sudden along comes this shocking question about a popular, veteran teacher: Is he gay or isn't he?

The idea for the movie came from the speech that Tom Hanks gave when he won the Academy Award for best actor for *Philadelphia*. I'm not sure who keeps track of such statistics, but I'm pretty sure *In & Out* is the only full-length feature film based on an Oscar acceptance speech. That just goes to show you how good a public speaker Hanks is—or more like how much practice he's had accepting acting trophies.

In the speech, Hanks paid tribute to his real life high school acting teacher, who was already out of the closet. But that got the satirists thinking: What if a movie star outed his teacher before the proverbial billion people watching the Oscars? That could certainly prove problematic for the entire school, particularly the principal.

This was much harder than playing the principal in those John Hughes films whose toughest job is dealing with the angst of pimple-faced kids. In *In & Out*, there was a teacher who was about to be married who was gay. He had been outed on national TV by his prized acting student, and the straightlaced school was under siege from tabloid reporters.

When director Frank Oz called to offer me the role of the principal, he was selling me all the way. "I really want you for this role. I'm not going to tell you it's funny, you know it's funny," he said.

I wanted to work on the movie because I immensely admired Frank and his films like *Little Shop of Horrors* and *Dirty Rotten Scoundrels,* as well as Kevin Kline, who had already committed to play the teacher. But I had a dilemma. My granddaughter had just been born, and she was coming to visit me in Los Angeles at the same time the movie would be shooting in New York.

"Frank, I have a problem," I told him. "My granddaughter is coming down from San Francisco, so I have the choice of either waking up in the morning and seeing your face, or waking up in the morning and seeing my granddaughter's face. It's no reflection on you, but I'd rather see my granddaughter's face than yours."

Not only did Frank make the schedule and have me home in time for my granddaughter's arrival, he did it in spite of the fact that I had come down with the flu and missed a week of shooting. Maybe he was just tired of seeing my face every morning.

•

I also played the President of the United States in the movie *First Family.* I didn't model President Manfred Link on any particular president. I borrowed traits from four different presidents: the use of power of Lyndon

Johnson, the pettiness of Richard Nixon, the humanity of Gerald Ford, and the folksiness of Jimmy Carter.

Actually, President Link was the submarine commander promoted a few grades and then elected almost by chance. In fact, he became president through the back door. A week before the election, the favorite candidate was shot, so he stepped in to fill the slot on the ballot and was elected. Not surprisingly, he was unprepared for the task.

The movie took a weird turn along the way from script to screen. It was originally about nuclear energy falling into the wrong hands, but it ended up being about large vegetables that are tainted by radioactivity. I don't think the audience was able to establish the connection between the large vegetables and a clear and present danger to society. Suffice it to say, this was not *Dr. Strangelove*, with the threat being the end of the world as we know it; that's about as big as it gets.

So in the scheme of movie presidents, Michael Douglas in *The American President* and Kevin Kline in *Dave* would be considered two-termers like Ronald Reagan and Bill Clinton. My President Link was more like William Henry Harrison, who got sick on inauguration day and died a month later.

On the other end of the power scale, I played an elf in the aptly titled comedy *Elf.* Actually, I was Papa Elf and Will Ferrell was my adopted son. You'd think this would be a badge of honor for my grandchildren, what with me playing a toymaker and all, but kids have no sense of irony.

For instance, they will be having Oreo cookies. You'll tell them that they are going to turn into an Oreo if they eat another one, to which they defiantly respond: "No, I won't. I could never turn into an Oreo cookie."

Or I'll explain to my granddaughter Taylor that she is nine and I'm seventy-five, which makes me eight times as old as her.

"Taylor, you will have to do all the birthdays you've had in your life eight times to be as old as Poppy," I'll say.

She'll think for a minute and then say something like, "But I haven't had my birthday this year, and I want a cookies 'n' cream ice cream cake."

So for my granddaughter Annabella, my playing a character is a tough concept to grasp. She can't quite put it together.

"You are Bob Newhart," she'll say.

"Yes," I tell her.

"But you're also Poppy. . . ."

"Yes, I am."

"And you're an elf."

Yep.

•

Now that I have mentioned two of my grandchildren, I need to mention the other five: Maddie, Caroline, William, Timothy, and Griffin.

CHAPTER TEN

Smoking and Drinking

For most of my life I was a chain-smoker. In nearly every photograph we have from the fifties, sixties, and seventies, I'm holding a cigarette. I always smoked onstage, as did many other performers in those days. I was so addicted that if I woke up at night to go to the bathroom, I'd light a cigarette to smoke on the walk.

Smoking is absurd, if you really think about. That was the premise of my routine "Introducing Tobacco to Civilization." In the routine, Sir Walter Raleigh calls the head of the West Indies Company in England from the colonies to tell him about a new find called "tobacco."

The uses of tobacco are not obvious. Think about listening to someone try to explain tobacco who is not familiar with it:

It's a kind of leaf... and you bought eighty tons of it! Let me get this straight. You bought eighty tons of leaves.... It isn't that kind of leaf. What is it, a special food or something?... It has a lot of different uses. Like what?... Are you saying, "snuff?" What's snuff?... That's when you take a pinch of tobacco and shove it up your nose... and sometimes it makes you sneeze. I imagine it would!... It has some other uses. You can chew it, put it in a pipe, or shred it and roll it in a piece of paper. You stick the rolled paper between your lips and you light it on fire.... When it starts burning, you inhale the smoke! It seems you could get the same effect from standing in front of a fireplace.

Consider that this routine appears in the filings of the court record in the landmark tobacco industry litigation undertaken by the federal government against the tobacco companies—in two different places.

•

I starred in an anti-smoking movie called *Cold Turkey*, which was written and directed by Norman Lear of *All in the Family* fame. The premise of the 1971 movie was that a tobacco company would put up $25 million to any town that could quit smoking for an entire month.

Led by Reverend Brooks (played by Dick Van Dyke), the fictitious town of Eagle Rock, Iowa, populated with 4,006 heavy smokers, takes up the challenge. My job, as Merwin Wren, the PR man from the tobacco company, was to keep the town smoking, because we reasoned that it would be bad for business if an entire town could kick the habit. It was, as the movie's tagline put it, "The battle of the butts."

The message of the movie didn't faze me a bit. I smoked during filming, and so did most of the people on location in Greenfield, Iowa—despite the fact that the city's real town council had voted to ban smoking just before production began.

My realization about the evils of nicotine came one summer day in 1985 when I developed a nosebleed that just wouldn't stop. Of course, Ginnie did what every wife would do under the circumstances: She called her gynecologist. Actually, he was a close friend of ours, Maurie Lazarus, and he told us to go immediately to the nearest hospital.

We were at our house in Malibu with the girls, Jennifer, who was fourteen, and Courtney, who was eight. So after Ginnie had arranged for my manager, Arthur, and his wife, Patty, to watch the girls, we were off in an ambulance to St. John's in Santa Monica.

It turned out I had a condition called polycythemia secondary. It's like the reverse of leukemia. Due to excess nicotine in my bloodstream, my body was overproducing red blood cells, thereby causing the uncontrollable nosebleed. The doctor explained that if I had not reached the hospital as quickly as I did, I could have died.

Before I was out of intensive care, the tabloids had gotten hold of the story and were bombarding MTM and my home with phone calls. The PR man from MTM, Larry Bloustein, fielded one call from a tabloid reporter. Larry assured the reporter that I was fine and had a severe nosebleed and was just taking some time off. The reporter stopped him in midsentence with a chilling revelation.

"Larry," he said. "I have a copy of Bob's hospital records right in front of me and it states that he has polycythemia secondary." Which, of course, was true. But, thankfully, the secondary type is nowhere near as severe as primary polycythemia.

Obviously, I had to stop smoking. Not being able to quit cold turkey, I started using one of those kits that lets you down easy with nicotine patches. With the patch glued be-hind my ear, I would buy a pack of cigarettes and dump half the pack into the trash. A few weeks later, I increased my dumping to three-quarters of the pack. Once I got down to four cigarettes a day, I reasoned that there wasn't much difference between four cigarettes and none.

So I've stopped smoking, but I still drink. And I'm a pretty good drunk, too. I mean, I *play* a pretty good drunk.

•

I am three-quarters Irish and one-quarter German, which makes me a very meticulous drunk. My father's side was half Irish, half German, my mother is full Irish. Come to think of it, I don't know of any German comedians. Most Germans don't have a sense of humor. They are very lit-eral. Someone once said that more funny things are said at a cocktail party in Paris than in an entire year in Germany.

I've found that the interesting thing about a drunk is that the drunk thinks that he is the only one who knows he's drunk. He thinks he's really putting it over on the other people and that they are not aware that he's bombed. To him, there is no reason to suspect that he has had five martinis even though he might h-h-h-have tr-tr-tr-ouble en-n-n-n-nunciating.

Of course, you realize that you have been overserved when you wake up with a hangover. Here's a guy from a routine I wrote who has the daddy of all hangovers. When he comes downstairs the following morning, his seven-year-old son is playing with his toys.

Rob, don't play with the dump truck, just leave the dump truck alone.... Don't play with the vroom toy, just leave the vroom toy alone. Daddy doesn't feel well. Daddy has a cold, Robert. . . . Another cold. Yes, I know . . . I know Daddy had a cold last weekend. Grown-ups get weekend colds. . . . You get a cold from going from a warm place into a cold place and from a cold place to a warm place . . . and from booze, yes. Who told you you could get it from booze? That's where Mommy said Daddy's colds come from? Have Mommy come in—and don't slam the door.

His wife walks into the room.

Hi dear. . . . I feel fine. I know I was drinking last night. I'm just sitting here watching television. . . . Picture tube's been out a week, huh? God, I thought I was going blind. . . . Yes, yes, I know I have your dress on, dear. You don't have to tell me. . . . That's why the milkman waved at me this morning. It didn't make a hell of a lot of sense at the time. . . . What does Fred want for breakfast? Who the hell is Fred? . . . My old army buddy. I insisted he stay with us last night. Honey, I was never in the army. How the hell could I have an old army buddy named Fred?

Then they talk about his schedule for the day.

I thought I'd sit here for a while and then maybe in a couple hours I thought I'd try to make it to that chair over there. If that goes well, I thought I would try to stand up tomorrow.

•

I'll never forget when I experienced the daddy of all hangovers while filming *Catch-22*. As I mentioned earlier, we were shooting in a small pueblo in Mexico called Guaymas. To reach Guaymas, you fly from Los Angeles to Tucson, Arizona, change planes to Hermosillo, Mexico, and then drive two hours to Guaymas.

As if the isolated location wasn't enough to make us hit the cantina, Mike Nichols had called all of us together at the beginning of filming and explained our collective roles in the film. The cast was an eclectic mix: Orson Welles, Martin Balsam, Art Garfunkel, Martin Sheen, Jon Voight, Norman Fell, Richard Benjamin, and Bob Balaban. Mike informed us, "You people don't exist. You are purely figments of Captain Yossarian's imagination."

By his actions, Orson seemed to disagree. He kept trying to direct Mike. After a take of a scene, Welles would turn to Mike and say, "There's your cut, Mike." Mike would reply, "Thank you, Orson, but I'm going to make a cut somewhere else."

Mike saw us as the Greek chorus whose purpose was to underscore the catch-22: You can't get out because you don't want to fly, and only insane people would fly under these conditions, so, therefore, you are not insane as long as you want to get out. Which is how a lot of us felt about the reality of our situation.

Major Major, the character I play, is a paranoid commander who is in over his head. Though he's been promoted to major, he wanted to stay lieutenant because being a major carried too much responsibility. He refuses to meet people. His orderly was told to only admit people into his office for a meeting when he wasn't there. When he was there, no one was to enter until he snuck out the window.

One night after a typically long, hot, and confusing day, Marty Balsam, Norm Fell, and I were throwing back the drinks. I wasn't on the schedule to work the next day, so I didn't think much about my intake. Before long, I was overserved.

Somehow the schedule changed and I ended up in the first scene the next morning. In the scene, Dick Benjamin and I were burying somebody. Tony Perkins, who played the minister, was offering a prayer for the dead. Yossarian was up in a tree, naked. With every line, my head pounded harder and my cottonmouth worsened. It was hotter than hell in the baking sun. I prayed that nobody would blow their lines. I just wanted the scene to end so I could go back to my trailer and take a nap.

About two weeks later, Mike Nichols called me into the production office. He showed me the scene from the day I was hungover. Watching it unfold, I felt nauseous all over again. When the reel stopped, he told me: "This is the quality I'm looking for in Major Major."

I didn't say a word. I wanted to tell him that I couldn't do that every night for him. No matter how privileged I was to be in the movie, I couldn't get blotto every night to produce the hangover that brought Major Major out of me. But I couldn't summon the courage to tell him.

•

Every night for years, I played a drunk in my routine "The Retirement Party." His name was Charlie Bedlow, an accountant who was retiring after fifty years on the job. At Charlie's retirement party, his pompous bosses reward his years of crunching numbers in a small cubicle with insincere speeches and that standard parting gift—a cheap watch. When it was time for Charlie to speak, he slurred his words and spoke the sober truth.

Golly, I've been sitting here listening to Mr. Clay-ton, Mr. Tib-ton and, of course, Bruce here, and through their speeches one thought kept recurring in my mind—I think I'm going to throw up. I have never heard such drivel in all my life. I don't suppose that it ever occurred to any one of you that I had to get half stoned every morning to make it down to this crummy job. You'd be smiling and easygoing if you were gassed all the time, too.

A lot of people have asked me, "Charlie, what are you going to do when you finally retire? Are you going to get a little part-time job in Florida, or just loll around the beach?" In other words, what am I going to do? I have some tapes from some office parties that I am going to let go for fifteen hundred bucks a copy. Let me take that back a minute. The June picnic may run seventeen-five. And with the money I make off the tapes and Miss Wilson's hundred thou, I should do pretty good.

I can imagine how he felt because I had seen people just like him at the various accounting jobs I held. I received a letter from someone who was upset at the drunken accountant routine because he felt I was mocking the nameless, faceless corporate workers of the world. I wrote back and explained that I was not making fun of Charlie Bedlow; I was making fun of the system that made him an alcoholic. I was mocking his dehumanizing job. The only way the poor guy could make it through the day was to be soused.

•

The producers of *The Bob Newhart Show* had seen me onstage as Charlie Bedlow, so they knew I could play a drunk. Occasionally they asked me to go to that well. Once

I got drunk with the Peeper, bought a horse, and brought it into my apartment as a baby gift. But it was another very funny episode that I believe helped create the drinking game that ties me to Trivial Pursuit: "Hi, Bob!"

In the episode, Jerry, Howard, Mr. Carlin, and I are sitting around watching a football game. Every time Jerry's team scores, we pass around a jug of booze. It was a high-scoring game and by the fourth quarter, we're all blotto.

When I go to the phone to order Chinese food from the House of Hu, all I can muster is "moo goo gai pan," which I proceed to repeat over and over again. After the guys all sing a rendition of "Over the River and Through the Woods," Emily arrives home from a trip a day early. I greet her with a drunkenly goofy, "Hi, Emily. What's happening?" From the couch, Mr. Carlin chimes in, "Where's the Chinese food?"

The game "Hi, Bob!" is similar, only without the Chinese food. Several friends gather around the TV and watch *The Bob Newhart Show* reruns. Every time someone says, "Hi, Bob," you take a drink of your favorite alcoholic beverage. My only advice: If you play the game, stay in the dorm, the den, or the rec room at the retirement home, and don't drive home afterward.

According to a 1982 story in the *New York Times*— I guess it was a slow news day—the game started when the show went into reruns. I later heard that it originated at Southern Methodist University in Dallas. SMU is, I'm told, a party school, so this is possible.

Comedians dish it out, so they have to be able to take it. While I prefer charades or Monopoly, I've come to realize that the game people are most likely to associate with me is the drinking game "Hi, Bob!"

The second time I hosted *Saturday Night Live,* Chris Farley and David Spade played "Hi, Bob!" I was in a sketch, and when people walked into the sketch and greeted me with a "Hi, Bob," they would throw one down.

I only hope that I won't go down in history for creating the most hangovers on college campuses. Being the Jack Daniel's of show business is not exactly what I want to be remembered for.

CHAPTER ELEVEN

The Science of Humor

I'm not a fan of books that examine humor in a scientific fashion. If I ever see another book called *The Serious Side of Comedy*, I'm going to throw up. I feel like comedy is that tribe in Africa who doesn't want their pictures taken because they believe a photograph steals part of their soul. The closer you get to understanding humor, the more you begin to lose your sense of humor.

Comedy is a way to bring logic to an illogical situation, of which there are many in everyday life. I've always likened what I do to the man who is convinced that he is the last sane man on Earth. This guy is something like the Paul Revere of psychotics running through the town and yelling, "This is crazy!" But no one pays attention to him.

A long time ago, I read a news item that illustrates this point nicely. An engineer at a Palm Springs TV station had a private porno tape that he was playing for his buddies on the late shift. Somehow, he accidentally transmitted the tape over the air. The strange thing was that the station didn't receive a single telephone call while the tape was playing, but the minute it was over, the phone lines lit up with outraged callers.

I decided to do a routine based on this. Picture a guy sitting at home when all of a sudden a porno movie comes on his TV. His wife, who is in the other room, tells him she's going up to bed.

"Okay, sweetheart," he says. "You go ahead. I'll be there soon. I'm just watching the end of this movie."

"What movie are you watching?" she yells from the staircase.

"I don't know what the name of the movie is, but the girl is very good. . . ."

"Who's in it?" she says.

"Nobody we know . . . no stars. . . . Wow this new girl is something else."

Then, when the tape ends, he calls the station to ask how they could air such smut.

•

When I started out in the sixties, there was a sea change in comedy. The traditional stand-up comics like Henny Youngman and Milton Berle were doing mother-in-law jokes and one-liners about their wives being bad cooks. They were standard in-and-out jokes. It was "Take my wife, please."

I was part of that change that shook up the dull Eisenhower years, along with Shelley Berman, Mike and Elaine, Jonathan Winters, and, of course, Lenny Bruce. I say of course, because Lenny was the only one of us who went to jail for his art.

Generally speaking, ours was a different kind of comedy than telling jokes. We did situational comedy. We told stories and did comedic vignettes. *Time* magazine dubbed us the "sick comics" because our stories poked at supposedly sacred topics. I was dealing with a revered ex-president, Abraham Lincoln. Shelley did a bit on the taboo topic of suicide. Mike and Elaine did a funeral routine that was hilarious. A sample: "We have three caskets. Mahogany for $1,500. Oak for $750. And for $15 we put him outside in a box and god knows what happens to him."

Our audience was equally nontraditional. College kids made up our fan base. Nightclubs were expensive. There was a cover charge, and then they had to pay for drinks. Near as I could determine, "Take my wife, please" had no relevance to them. So the college kids ordered pizza and beer and sat around listening to comedy records. Our comedy albums became their nightclubs.

My influences came from the more absurdist side of life. I've never forgotten the time I heard that this lady in Britain published her correspondence with Winston Churchill, so Robert Benchley decided to publish his correspondence with George Bernard Shaw. Benchley's correspondence consisted of letters accusing Shaw of taking his umbrella at the theater and asking for it to be returned. Shaw kept writing back saying, "I don't know who you are, and I don't have your umbrella."

Some comedians of my era worked successfully in that old style of one-liners. Rodney Dangerfield was one: "My wife is so neat that I got up to go to the bathroom and I came back and the bed was made," or "My wife's driving me crazy. She loves it when I talk dirty during sex. Last night, she called from a motel . . ."

The new comedians put our own personal stamps on our routines. You can steal a one- or two-line joke. A lot of comedians would see a comedian and move on to the next town and do half of his routine. I'll never forget watching a Scottish comedian come onstage and do Phyllis Diller's act. But you can't steal part of "The Driving Instructor." Our material was unique to each of us.

•

Comedy has changed again since the sixties, as the once acceptable limits of raunchy humor have been breached, but audiences have changed, too. We have lost our ability to laugh at ourselves.

I don't have a joke on albino cross-dressers, but if I did, I guarantee you that I would receive a letter from the local chapter of the ACD asking me to cease and desist making fun of albino cross-dressers.

If I start to tell certain jokes, I can hear people in the audience cringing because they are afraid I am going to cross the line.

The problem is that we live an uptight country. Why don't we just laugh at ourselves? We are funny. Gays are funny. Straights are funny. Women are funny. Men are funny. We are all funny, and we all do funny things. Let's laugh about it.

I've made a few changes to my act. I did quit wearing a tuxedo long ago because a tux meant going to work. When

Bill Cosby first appeared onstage in a sweater, the rules on attire began to relax—though Rickles still wears a tux. I've shortened a few of my older routines to adapt to the limited attention span of audiences. Also, in the old days, I used to smoke a cigarette while doing "Abe Lincoln." Now I use a cell phone.

However, in the past ten years, I've learned that some things need a little explanation. Each time I start "The Driving Instructor" with the line "Imagine I'm a driving instructor and seated next to me is a woman driver," there is an audible reaction from the audience.

"Okay," I tell the women in the audience, "you must feel this is a sexist routine because it's a woman driver. That was certainly never my intention when I wrote and performed this for the first time some forty-five years ago. Mrs. Webb is one of my dearest friends. But if some of you are offended, I will make it a Chinese driver."

Then, I begin performing the routine in faux Chinese. After the laughter dies down, I explain that I can do eight more minutes of Chinese, or I can make it a woman driver.

I'll admit that sometimes comedians can be a little insensitive.

The first time I hosted *Saturday Night Live* was on May 10, 1980. In one of the many sketches we rehearsed during the week, I played a Union officer. One of the men in my company had been killed and I kept forgetting to write a condolence letter to his mother. Everywhere I turned, something would remind me of the letter.

"Do you want some lettuce?" someone would ask.

Lettuce.... letter.

The night the showed aired, I dressed in Union military blues, and we performed the sketch. No one laughed. It just laid there, dead onstage. It's not surprising. That was the night after Jimmy Carter had launched a military rescue effort to free the American hostages in Iran, and a U.S. military helicopter had crashed in the failed effort.

Somehow, we didn't make the connection until after the show.

•

One of the dangers of becoming successful as a comedian— and I mean successful beyond that $1.18 in quarterly royalties coming in from sales of *The Button-Down Mind of Bob Newhart*—is that you become cut off from your source material. I no longer work part-time jobs, so that's a loss of source material right there. As soon as you make enough money, you hire a business manager to balance the books and file form 4887 with the IRS.

Now when I'm on a plane or in the lounge at an airport, I try to eavesdrop on other people's conversations to stay in touch with everyday life. Not only do I feel cut off, even the people I'm around sometimes seem cut off.

Valet parking, a subject often suggested to me, probably wouldn't work, though parking lots might. Lately I've noticed that the entry-level job for the people who have escaped from the poorest countries is the parking attendant. Determining his accent gives you a real insight into the next trouble spot in the world. His brother came over from his country and then sent for him.

"All you have to do is say, 'You going to a movie. . . . Tree dollars,' " the guy tells his brother. "That's all you have to know."

Problem is, what if I pulled in and said my wife's expecting a baby, she just broke her water, and we have to get her to the nearest hospital!

"You going to a movie. . . . Tree dollars."

Becoming a senior citizen has given me a few universal jokes that any audience can appreciate, like the man who was slowly losing his hearing. The man said to his friend, "I just got this new hearing aid and it's great."

"How much did it cost you?" his friend asks.

"One hundred and fifty bucks," the man with the new hearing aid says.

"Wow," his friend says. "That's a great deal. What kind is it?"

"It's 4:15."

•

Success has given me the opportunity to embarrass myself in different forums. In the past several years, I've had some unusual offers that I've accepted. Either I want to be more unpredictable, or just more perverse.

In a stamps.com commercial, I played Frank Mettman Jr. Frank explains that since the founding of the Mettman Manufacturing Company in 1942, the Mettman name has become synonymous with ill-conceived products that carry the risk of serious physical injury, like the Suckmaster 100 vacuum cleaner, the rocking folding recliner, and the unfortunate home surgery kit.

As Frank talks, people are shown using these various products and injuring themselves in bizarre and painful ways.

But, Frank adds, there has been some progress. The company signed up for a new service called stamps.com that allows you to download your postage directly to your printer. This has saved the company lots of time when it needs to respond to people who have been injured by its various products.

I thought the commercial was offbeat and funny, and it won the Palme d'Or for commercials.

Before stamps.com, I had done several in-house training videos for IBM. One of them was in the vein of "Introducing Tobacco to Civilization." I played Herman Hollerith, who came up with the punch card for clocking in workers. Herman was trying to explain the new system he had come up with to rid the company of idiotic jargon and force the engineers to speak in plain English. The ad agency had neglected to tell me that it was tongue-in-cheek. So I was having the hardest time getting the lines out.

"We are all familiar with the cyclomilitron and interfacing it with diobionetics . . ."

I would blow a word and hear, "Okay, Herman Hollerith, take twelve!" Which was making it worse. About the fifteenth take, I realized that I was speaking gobbledygook and it wasn't supposed to make any sense. I had been playing it straight.

And they say comedians are perverse.

I was also asked to give a commencement address at my son's alma mater, Catholic University in Washington, D.C., in 1997. My son Tim had graduated in 1989 with a degree in English literature specializing in the poetry of Yeats. As you all know, when you pick up the classified pages you just see page after page of jobs for Yeats scholars.

The graduates greeted me with a rousing, "Hi, Bob!"

"In preparation for the speech," I told them, "I read a number of other commencement addresses. There always seems to be an obligatory reference to Aldous Huxley's *Brave New World.* And also the need to give the perception that you are intelligent. You don't actually have to *be* intelligent, but just need to create the perception. This can usually be accomplished by a reference to Kafka—even if you haven't read any of his . . . or her works."

Thankfully, I got some laughs.

Then there is *Desperate Housewives*, which is either a serious drama or spoof depending on which side of the humor scale you fall. In what was perhaps the oddest and most flattering offer I've received in recent memory, I was asked to guest star on the show as a character named Morty, the estranged ex-boyfriend of Susan's mother (played by Lesley Ann Warren, no less). Teri Hatcher, of course, is Susan.

I was thrilled with the offer because it seems that most adults in the free world watch it every week. The show is one of the hottest things on TV, and they really could have gotten most anyone for my part. They could've gotten Bruce Willis if they wanted, or even the governor of California.

To me, the show is a spoof on a soap opera and makes fun of the genre that encompasses *Soap* and *Dynasty.* However, I find that most people watch it as a soap opera and aren't aware that it's a send-up. I know people who are such fanatics that they plan their week around the show.

They wouldn't dare tape it or TiVo it, as the case is these days, because they wouldn't be able to call their friends immediately after the show and gossip.

I did see one episode that had a truly memorable scene. In the show, one of the housewives follows the plumber, with whom she is having an affair and who is cheating on their affair. She hangs back a distance of five or six car-lengths and soon loses him. Finally, she sees a car that looks like his, so she walks up to it and confronts the man and woman. After apologizing for a case of mistaken identity, she returns to her car.

The girl in the car says to the man, "Was that your wife?"

He looks at her and says, "If that was my wife, do you think I'd be here with you?"

CHAPTER TWELVE

You Can Have
My Frequent-Flier Miles

Good Evening, I'd like to welcome you aboard the Mrs. Grace L. Ferguson Airline (and Storm Door Company). I don't know how much you know about our airlines. We've only been in business about a week. Our airline was founded on the premise that what the American public wanted was low-cost overseas transportation. We've attempted to eliminate what we call in the airline business "frills and extras"... like maintenance and radar and a whole bunch of technical instruments.... Have you ever had one that hangs on for about four or five days? I don't mind the headache so much, but it's that damn double vision....

•

I really dislike flying, and there's a logical explanation for this. The first airline flight I ever took was a non-scheduled flight on Costal Cargo. It was 1952, and I was on my way to Camp Roberts in California to serve my two years in the military. The plane was a C-47 cargo

CHAPTER TWELVE

You Can Have
My Frequent-Flier Miles

Good Evening, I'd like to welcome you aboard the Mrs. Grace L. Ferguson Airline (and Storm Door Company). I don't know how much you know about our airlines. We've only been in business about a week. Our airline was founded on the premise that what the American public wanted was low-cost overseas transportation. We've attempted to eliminate what we call in the airline business "frills and extras"... like maintenance and radar and a whole bunch of technical instruments.... Have you ever had one that hangs on for about four or five days? I don't mind the headache so much, but it's that damn double vision....

•

I really dislike flying, and there's a logical explanation for this. The first airline flight I ever took was a nonscheduled flight on Costal Cargo. It was 1952, and I was on my way to Camp Roberts in California to serve my two years in the military. The plane was a C-47 cargo

The invention of the airplane changed society forever. In the telephone routine titled "Merchandising the Wright Brothers," which I wrote while trying to fill *The Button-Down Mind*, the Wright Brothers are marketing their first plane to a guy from a sales-promotion firm, who is pushing to start booking passengers immediately. Of course, there are a few problems.

"In all of the pictures we have," the sales guy tells Orville, "either you or Wilbur is lying on the wings. Now ... if we're going to charge them seventy-five or eighty bucks to the coast, I don't know how they'll go for lying on the wings like that. . . . And having to land every 105 feet."

I'm not sure about flying on the wing, but truthfully I didn't mind the old propeller jets because I prefer a lot of noise when I fly. Now they have those pod engines hanging from the wings. When I hear them hissing, I sit there and say to myself, "They're probably on. They must be. Yes, I'm certain they're on."

Before takeoff, the crew always runs down a checklist. I'm convinced that this has nothing to do with maintenance or safety. It's just to make the passengers feel better. The list is read by a flight attendant or the pilot, whoever happens to be flying the plane that day.

First, they come out and kick the tires. This is reassuring. After that, they walk around the plane and count the engines—one, two, three, four, check. I don't mind that too much, except when they check it against the list on the clipboard they are carrying.

Each time I fly, I like to treat it as a new adventure. I relish the technological achievements of man inventing

and perfecting the airplane. I'll turn to the person next to
me and say something along the lines of, "This flying is
amazing. The people down there look like ants."

Usually, they'll respond with something like, "Those
are ants, you idiot. We haven't taken off yet."

•

*Incidentally, I want to apologize for your having to stand
all the way. If I can give you a little tip, every half hour or
so you want to alternate your arms through those straps
above your head. You folks flying tourist class, you don't
have any straps so don't bother looking for them. We're going to have a little drill in a few moments by our two stew-
ardesses, Trixie and Bubbles.... I'm sorry, Miss Swanson
and Miss Savage ... and they'll show you how to put your
life jackets on. There really isn't that much to it, but a lot of
people get them on backward and that way you are going
to wind up with your face in the water. If we should have to
ditch, you'll have plenty of warning because our copilot becomes hysterical. He'll start running up and down the
aisles yelling, "We're going to crash." Actually, he gets
kind of panicky, and it isn't always easy to understand
him. At least it has been in the past anyway. If you see him
running up and down the aisles, and you can't make out
what he's saying, you might slip on your life jackets to be
on the safe side....*

•

The two airlines I prefer are Delta and United, mainly because I'm not a stockholder in either one.

I like Delta because they pay their pilots the most out of

all the U.S. airlines, and there's nothing better at 30,000 feet than a happy pilot. On United, I can listen to the pilots talking to the air-traffic controllers on the in-flight entertainment system. That way, I know exactly when the turbulence will begin and end, and I can mentally prepare myself. At least I feel like I'm doing something besides sitting there and waiting for an air pocket to turn my drink over onto my lap.

Regardless of which airline I fly, I prefer to sit by the window so I can see what's going on outside. I want to know if we are flying over the Grand Canyon or into it.

·

Considering I've flown something like two million miles in my life, I haven't had that many bad experiences— though I take little comfort in this because it only takes one. Once I was on a DC-10 leaving LAX, and one of the wing flaps didn't retract. The pilots circled back and dumped fuel while the passengers braced against the seats in front of us. It was scary, but everything ended up fine.

Another time, Ginnie and I were flying from Paris to London with the Rickleses. As we were coming in, Ginnie whispered to me, "We're awfully high."

"Yeah, I know," I said, pressing my nose to the window.

"We're too high to land," she reiterated.

"Yeah, I, I know."

"We're not going to land."

With that, the pilot gunned the engines, and the plane banked hard to the right. Barbara Rickles, who was sitting across the aisle reading a magazine, looked up and nonchalantly said to Don, "We're going up again."

Ginnie let out a scream and Don said, "Newhart, can't you do something with your wife?" and went back to reading. I turned to Ginnie and said, "It's like flying with Chauncey Gardner and his wife." (Chauncey was the trusting childlike character Peter Sellers portrayed in *Being There.*)

•

I'd like to answer some questions that you may have about the airline.... Ma'am ... if I may, I'll repeat the question so everyone can hear it. If we should ditch, how long will the plane remain afloat? That's your question, ma'am? Uh, golly that's awful hard to say, ma'am. Some of 'em go down like a rock. And then, for some reason or another, others will stay up for two or three minutes.... I want to get to the gentleman way in the back. If you could speak up, I can't hear you over the roar of our engines. Oh, wait, they've stopped now. Harry, the engines are going out.... Try the third button on the left, I think Harry ... hold it. Harry, the cabin lights went out. Try the third button on the right. That's got 'em. You want to try the question again? ... Sir, I'm sorry, I still can't make out what you're saying.... Sure, if you want to try it that way, it may work.... First word, sounds like running, sounds like racing ... track and field ... ran ... It sounds like ran ... man....A lot of man ...A whole bunch of ... men.... Oh, men! It's right behind you, sir. I'm glad I took your question ahead of this gentleman's over here.

•

The pilot episode of *The Bob Newhart Show* centered on fear of flying. Titled "Fly the Friendly Skies," the story line involved a group of my patients who are afraid to fly. I plan a trip to New York for them and decide that Emily should come along, too.

Next, I invite my pilot neighbor Howard Borden, played by Bill Daily, to speak to the group. I tell them that he has been a navigator for fifteen years and logged some twenty-five million miles on big jets without incident. Unfortunately, Howard's nervousness compounds their anxiety.

Howard is not much of pilot, as we learn in a different episode.

"I'm taking the practical part of my copilot test, you know, where I actually fly the plane," he tells Emily.

"Well, haven't you been studying?" Emily asks.

"Yeah, I know about wind vectors and about stress analysis and transponder codes. There's only one principle in aerodynamics that puzzles me," he says.

"What's that?

"What holds the plane up?"

What I don't realize is that Emily is scared to fly. Finally, I figure this out and confront her about it.

"You're afraid of flying?"

"That's what I said."

"Well, honey, that's just stupid."

"Do you tell those people in your workshop who are terrified of flying that they're stupid?"

"Well, of course not, honey. But I don't love them."

•

I really have to get back in the cabin now. We have it on automatic pilot but the damn thing keeps kicking in and out all the time, and we never really know if it's on or not. Oh, one of the reasons I came out here, I nearly forgot—have any of you ever been to Hawaii before? This gentleman right here. It's kind of liver shaped isn't it, sir?...Sir, as we're coming in, would you mind very much stopping by the cabin and pointing it out to us?

•

The service on airplanes has gotten much worse since I started flying. The salary cutbacks and disappearing pensions due to the airlines' perpetual state of bankruptcy has made flight attendants grumpy. Instead of being asked whether you'd like to have chicken or pasta for dinner, the dialogue is much less friendly.

"Do you want dinner?"

"What are the choices?"

"Yes or no."

And that's in first class. In coach, it's worse.

"Coffee or tea?"

"Coffee, please."

"Wrong, the answer is tea."

Such a great number of airlines have gone out of business or fly in bankruptcy that they are all probably beginning to wish they were more like the Mrs. Grace L. Ferguson Airline (and Storm Door Co.). The principle there was that if the airline failed, they would always have the storm door company to fall back on.

CHAPTER THIRTEEN

Let's Take a Break for Some Golf

Some people see golf as a religion. You play on Sunday. It's frustrating. You often swear, but you are supposed to act gentlemanly. If you cheat, you can go to a confessional and ask for forgiveness. And oftentimes, the harder you try, the worse things turn out for you.

I once came home from shooting a lousy eighteen holes, and Ginnie asked me how I played.

"Terrible," I said. "I couldn't hit a ball out of my shadow. I'm so mad that I don't even want to talk about it."

"I thought you played golf to relax," she said.

"Ginnie, you don't know the first thing about golf. You don't play it to relax. You play it to get mad and motivated."

I know fine athletes who have taken up golf, only to find they're no good at it. They become frustrated because it looks easy and they think it should come naturally to them. My friend Tom Harmon was a Heisman Trophy winner for Michigan State in the fifties and later played pro football. I always outhit him on the golf course because I have a loose, relaxed swing. It drove him crazy. To him, there was no logical way I should be able to hit the ball farther than him. The more I outdrove him, the harder he would swing at the ball, which is completely counterproductive.

Golf was a great occupier of time on the road. When I played Vegas for weeks at a clip, I used to joke that golf saved my marriage because it gave me something to do besides get in trouble.

In the past year and a half, I haven't played any golf. My back bothers me when I play, and I don't hit the ball as far as I used to. Some people accept the fact that their game is degrading, but I can tell you it's about as much fun as miniature golf when your ball is constantly dropping short.

In my day, I was actually a pretty good golfer—a nine handicap. When I signed on to play the lead in the TV movie *The Sports Pages,* alongside four-time Emmy winner Kelsey Grammer, I had to do something that would make any weekend golfer shudder. I had to make my game worse.

My character was Doc Waddems, a guy who had never broken one hundred. As I mentioned, I have a textbook swing. Even the pro at my country club says I have a smooth swing. Anyone who knows anything about golf could see that if I used my normal swing, I'd break one hundred. The movie wouldn't be believable unless I altered my swing.

So I went to the driving range and watched guys with bad swings. I made a composite out of all the bad swings.

This was as close as I come to method acting. The funny thing is, it didn't mess up my game.

•

I'm not denigrating religion by comparing it to golf. As I said earlier, I was raised Catholic and attended Catholic schools all my life. My parents met at a church social. And my sister Mary Joan is a nun.

No kidding, though she's retired now.

There are odd things about being Catholic. In the Catholic religion, we have confession. Non-Catholics really don't understand the process of going into this little dark room and telling someone else all the terrible things we've done during the week. But if you are raised Catholic, there are certain tricks you learn: You sit in the very last pew, you watch the two lines move, and whichever line moves the fastest, that's the one you get into.

•

Enough religion. Back to golf.

The greater Los Angeles area has dozens of golf courses. Several of them are located on some of the most valuable ground in the United States. The Bel-Air Country Club, where I've been a member since 1961, is in one of the most expensive residential areas in the country, and so is Riviera. The L.A. Country Club occupies 200 acres on either side of Wilshire Boulevard in the Century City area, which is probably some of the most valuable commercial land in the universe. Nothing drives a developer crazier than a golf course located in areas like these. Nothing except the cemetery next door, that is.

There's also the Lakeside Country Club in the San Fernando Valley, which developed a reputation as a drinkers' club. I once played there with Gordon MacRae and George Gobel and saw why. We teed off at 8:30 A.M. On the third hole, they hopped into the golf cart and drove two fairways over for a couple of pops. When we reached the fifth, they went for another drink. By 10:00 A.M., they had hit three different refreshment stands.

The Bel-Air Country Club is very old Hollywood. Its legendary membership rolls have included Clark Gable, Howard Hughes, Dean Martin, and Jimmy Stewart, to name but a few. It's the club where Robert Wagner was caddying for Gable and Gable told him that he should be in pictures and gave Wagner a phone number to call. Now the regulars include James Garner, James Woods, Jack Nicholson, and Mike Connors.

Bel-Air is open to all races, creeds, and genders. Even women can now become full members on their own, rather than spouses of members. However, the club does occasionally vote down misfits. My friend Pierre Cossette, the producer, was one. Unfortunately, when Pierre was playing as a guest, he relieved himself behind the No. 1 green in the presence of the club president.

Pierre was not known for being particularly neat. He always had food stains on his clothes. One Christmas, I went to the Beverlycrest Cleaners and asked to buy a $50 gift certificate for Pierre. The manager said that they had never had a request for a gift certificate, but he agreed to create one.

After the urinating incident and the ensuing rejection of his application for membership, I called Pierre and told him that his friends were all embarrassed by what had happened. I further told him that I had gathered twelve of his closest friends, influential members, such as Andy Williams, Jerry Perenchio, and Jim Mahoney, to discuss the reason that Pierre was turned down by the club. He could then work on the problem and reapply in a year.

"Newhart, I'm really touched. That's one of the nicest things anyone has done for me," Pierre said. "What did you come up with?"

"Well, we came up with twelve different reasons."

The second time Pierre was nominated for membership, I wrote the club a letter on his behalf stating that the area where Pierre had relieved himself was now the site of a tree—and it was one of the prettiest trees on the entire course. Under these circumstances, I urged the membership committee to reconsider Pierre. They did, and he was accepted.

A certain private club in L.A. does not allow actors as members. Victor Mature was playing there, and he mused that he would like to join. When the member informed him that actors were not allowed, Mature quipped, "Have they seen any of my movies?"

I love playing at Bel-Air because you never know who you are going to run into. Once I was teeing up and George C. Scott asked if he could join me. On the third hole, he turned to me and said, "Explain to me how you do those telephone routines."

"Well, George, what I do is ask a question and then I

leave enough room to hear the answer in my head. Then I ask the next question."

"That's amazing," he said.

I thought to myself, no, George, playing *Patton* is amazing.

•

I stopped using a caddy a long time ago. Unlike John D. Rockefeller, who used to tip his caddy a dime, I'm not trying to save money. I don't mind spending $50 for someone to carry my clubs, but bad experiences have turned me off to their advice.

I was playing at Bel-Air one time and I had a caddy whose name was Dick. He was an out-of-work actor who acted very much like an actor-type. He spoke in a deep, basso profundo actorly voice.

A caddy is supposed to give you the line on a putt, how far out and how many cups to the left or right. Dick would give me these ridiculous lines. He'd say, "Mr. Newhart, I'd put that, oh, I'd say about an inch and three quarters on the right." Then I saw him on the course the following Monday, the day caddies are permitted to play, and he couldn't hit the ball worth a darn.

Another time I was playing in the L.A. Open Pro-Am at Riviera. I hadn't played the course that much so I asked my caddy what the line was off the tee, meaning: What should I aim for? He pointed to a eucalyptus tree in the distance. I hit the ball pretty well. As it took flight, the caddy mused, "Oh, that's good. That's real good. You couldn't have walked out there and placed the ball any better . . . great line . . . garden spot . . . sit down, ball! Sit down . . . whoa, stop! stop! . . . Oh, you better hit another one." My ball had landed solidly out of bounds.

Sam Snead knew how to handle a chatty caddy. One year when he was playing the L.A. Open, Sam hit a drive. He and his caddy walked to his ball. The caddy took a look and told Sam it was a hard five-iron or an easy four. Sam cut the caddy off.

"I'll club myself," Sam said. "All you do is carry the bag. That's your job. I don't want to hear you say anything."

They continued in silence until the eighteenth hole. Just as Sam was just about to hit his final approach shot of the day, the caddy spoke again.

"Mr. Snead—" he mumbled.

Sam cut him off. "I told you on the first hole, just carry the bag. I don't want any advice from you."

Sam parred the hole. As he was walking off the green, he turned to the caddy and asked, "What was so important that you had to tell me?"

"Mr. Snead, that wasn't your ball." A two-stroke penalty.

The greatest caddy stories I ever heard were about a caddy named Snake, who worked at Bel-Air. Snake was an alcoholic who stashed bottles of booze all over the course.

One day Snake was caddying for Dean Martin. At Bel-Air, the eleventh fairway parallels the fifteenth fairway. Dean putted out eleven and moved onto the twelfth tee. He turned to grab a club from Snake, but there was no Snake. Off in the distance, Dean saw Snake walking with his bag on the fifteenth fairway with another foursome.

Another time, Snake was out with Dean, and Dean hit one into the rough. Snake went looking for his ball. Five minutes passed and Dean called out to Snake, "Forget it,

I'll hit another one." Snake yelled back, "The hell with your ball, I can't find your bag."

•

Golf can be a very social game. Some of the most interesting conversations I've had were at the golf club. I remember hitting balls on the driving range at the L.A. Country Club once with Fred MacMurray. He was a lovely man, but both he and Bob Hope had reputations for being notoriously tight with their money because they grew up during the Depression. Their feeling was, you'd better watch your money because you could lose it all through no fault of your own.

It was 1972, and I was about to begin *The Bob Newhart Show*. Fred and I got to talking about his work schedule on *My Three Sons*. It was very lax. The show was in production for nine months, but Fred had a provision in his contract that he would tape all his scenes in three consecutive months.

Out of the blue, Fred volunteered to me that he was feeling guilty because he had worked only eighty days last year and had made $800,000 (which is like $40,000 a day in today's dollars). That stuck with me.

Several weeks later, my father-in-law, Bill Quinn, was doing a guest spot on Fred's show. They were sitting together, waiting for a scene to begin. Fred told Bill that Sunday had been a rough day because plumbing problems forced him to call a plumber.

"Do you know what plumbers get on Sunday?" Fred asked. "Forty-five dollars an hour." Fred paused. "Bill, you and I are in the wrong business."

•

There have been two great moments in golf for me. The first happened on the thirteenth hole at Bel-Air, which is a par three. I teed off and hit my first ball out of bounds, which is a two-shot penalty, and I put the next shot in the cup. It's the only time I ever hit the ball off the tee and into the hole. A perfect hole-in-three.

Undoubtedly, the highlight of my golf career was playing a round with Jack Nicklaus in a Pro-Am in Palm Springs. We teed off, and I hit my regular 200-yard drive, followed by my second shot. Jack got up and he hooked his ball in the woods. He was stymied, so on his second shot, he had to play it out 90 degrees. His ball ended up five yards behind mine.

Jack and I were both laying two, so I turned to him and said, "You're away, Jack," meaning that he would hit before me because he was farther from the hole. How often do you get to say that?

CHAPTER FOURTEEN

Famous People I've Met
(Including Don Rickles)

It happens to some of us: we are mistaken for someone famous. For me, it's Paul Newman. Sort of.

When people suddenly come upon me, they will occasionally blurt out, "Oh, Mr. Newman." They know it's New-something, so they soon pause and correct themselves. "Oh, I mean Mr. Newhart." I have attempted to use this to convince my wife that people think I look like Paul Newman. Her reply is always, "You don't bear the slightest resemblance to Paul Newman."

Some years ago, Ginnie and I were at Disneyland with our kids, Rob, Jennifer, and Courtney, and the Rickleses and their children, Mindy and Larry. As we were walking through the park, I turned to Ginnie and said, "Oh, great. People think I'm Paul Newman."

Ginnie shook her head. "Would you please cut that out?" she said. "You don't resemble him in any way. Now watch the kids, because I have to use the ladies' room."

When she was in the ladies' room, a young man came up to me. "Mr. Newhart," he said, "I love your show. Would you mind signing an autograph?"

"I'd be glad to," I replied. "But would you do me a favor? Just stand over by that bench, and when a redheaded woman comes out of the ladies' room, walk up to me and say, 'Mr. Newman, I loved you in *Hud*. Would you please sign an autograph?'"

On cue, as Ginnie walked out of the ladies' room, he ran over to me and did as I asked. Upon hearing the kid address me as Mr. Newman, and mention his affection for *Hud*, a puzzled look came across Ginnie's face. As we walked away, she kept shooting me glances of "I don't see the resemblance . . ."

Of course, after a forty-five-year career and more than fifteen seasons on network television, people do occasionally recognize me. The men think I'm an old army buddy and the women think I'm their first husband. Buck Henry once said that I'm the guy who has been at everybody's Thanksgiving dinner table.

Sometimes people will come up to me and say, "Wow, you sure look like Bob Newhart, but I guess you've been told that." My reply, "Yeah, I've heard that one before, fella." At that point, they usually put the voice and the face together.

I guess I just don't have that grabbing, leading-man look. I'm shorter than people think I am. I'm not actually any shorter than I am, but I am shorter than people think I am. If you must know, my hairline started receding when I was fifteen. It was probably from all the stress of watching my hair thin during the two preceding years.

The writers of my shows have used my lack of movie star looks for humor. In one episode of *The Bob Newhart Show*, Emily's dashingly handsome, wildly egotistical tennis pro laments to Bob, "You have no idea of the problems that we incredibly handsome people have to face." Bob ponders this, sighs, and says, "No, I suppose not."

Different writers, same joke a decade later on *Newhart*. The beautiful Julia Duffy says to me, "Frankly, being attractive can be a real burden. You don't know how lucky you are."

Or as Emily herself put it, "Bob, what I'm trying to say is that I just never went for those good-looking guys. That's why I married you."

But I did fight back in another episode when I told Emily, "This may come as a shock to you, but in high school, I was considered great looking."

Her response: "You're kidding!"

"I think it was my hair. I had great hair. I was the first kid in school to have a flat-top with a ducktail."

Before I went on television, I was often mistaken for a guy named Fred Neff, whom I've never met. People would drive by as I walked down the sidewalk and yell, "Yo, Fred, how are you? Why don't you give a call sometime." I would run alongside the car yelling, "I'm not Fred! I'm not Fred!"

Most of us have a double somewhere because there are only so many nose sizes, eyebrow thicknesses, and hairstyles to go around.

It's not a big problem to be mistaken for Paul Newman. It's strange being mistaken for Fred Neff, but that's not a problem, either. At least I don't get mistaken for Adolf Hitler.

Imagine the poor guy with a little mustache and a piece of hair falling in his face who does look like Hitler. Every time he gets on a plane, he knows he is going to get mistaken for Hitler. Inevitably, the seatmate will grow incredibly nervous. He'll greet the guy with "*Heil* . . . I mean hi . . ." He'll tell the Hitler look-alike he was just in St. Louis, seeing his buddies from World War II, but then he'll nervously backtrack. "We were all conscientious objectors. We didn't care who won. We didn't really follow the war all that closely."

•

If Dean Martin were alive, he would be laughing uncontrollably at the section you just read. I appeared on Dean's show twenty-four times, and he was the easiest person in the world to make laugh. Dean just liked to have a good time.

Dean never rehearsed. In fact, Dean didn't come into the studio all week. He only showed up on Sunday to do the show. The story went that NBC asked Dean to star in a variety show. In order to kill the idea without being too crass, Dean said yes, but that he would only come in one day a week. Instead of telling him that was impossible, the network agreed. So Dean would play an early round of golf and then appear around 1:00 P.M. on Sundays to do his show, because his feeling was that he wasn't going to blow an entire day doing television.

The guests rehearsed with his producer, Greg Garrison. Dean would sit in his dressing room, where he had a monitor showing the rehearsals. Sometimes he'd watch, other times he'd get caught up in a conversation about golf with the writers. Having not seen the rehearsals, he often had no idea where the routines were going, but he liked working without a net.

Once Dean played a store clerk and I played a man who was returning a very intimate gift from his wife, a toupee. From the moment I asked for a private room to discuss the return, Dean began smirking.

"Is it underwear?" he asked.

"No, it isn't underwear. My wife bought me a toupee for our anniversary, and I'd like to return it."

"Well, do you have it with you, sir?"

I furrowed my brow and pointed my eyes upward. "Under the hat . . ."

"What model is it, sir?"

"I don't know what model it is. . . . It's the crew cut with the widow's peak."

"Oh, our Mr. Wonderful model."

Dean was trying to stay in character, but I knew he wouldn't make it. He was desperately trying to hold back his laughter, but at this point it was becoming contagious. The entire routine was in danger of imploding. But I pressed on, which was like feeding minnows to a hungry shark.

I explained that I wanted to return the toupee because people were laughing at me because they knew it wasn't my real hair. "You see, we went to this party, and I bent down trying to put cheese dip onto a cracker and the toupee fell into the cheese dip. . . . Everybody stopped having cheese dip."

Dean was laughing so hard, tears formed in his eyes.

"It may be a laughing matter to you, sir, but it's not to me," I deadpanned. "The hostess started crying . . . and we spent about two hours trying to fish it out of the cheese dip. Anyway, I took it home and put it in our washer-dryer. . . . We have one of those with the window, you know. . . . Here's another problem. . . . The kids like to sit and watch it when it sticks to the glass so they're mad that I'm returning it."

"Would you like a full exchange?" Dean managed to spit out.

"I'd like a straight man who didn't laugh."

That one was pretty funny, but Dean also loved a gag I did that was as dry as beef jerky. Greg came to me and said that they needed a short bit to kick off a show, so I wrote a routine about a plate spinner.

On the air, I explained to Dean that I was from Eastern Europe and that I was a plate spinner in the circus. In my routine, I could spin five plates on the top of two sticks and keep them going for half an hour.

Dean asked me if I could show him. I explained that no, I couldn't because someone stole *"de plates on de plane and I only have sticks."* He asked me if I could do it anyway. I told him, *"Yea, I do vitout de plates."* So I launched into the plate spinning routine full-bore, intensely moving the sticks and pretending to juggle plates. It broke Dean up something fierce.

•

I met the Queen of England. It was 1964, and I was asked to come to London and give a command performance along with Lena Horne and Brenda Lee. My *Button-Down Mind* albums sold extremely well in London, owing to their reserved humor. When I told Ginnie about the invitation, the first thing she said was, "I have to buy a new dress."

We were living in New York at that time because I was starring in *The Entertainers*. We went dress shopping, and Ginnie narrowed it down to two dresses. One was priced at $400 and the other was $750. She asked me which one I liked. I told her to go for the $750. "How many times do you get to meet the queen?" I reasoned.

We flew to London, but the airport was fogged in so we were diverted to Frankfurt. The entire way from London to Frankfurt I was thinking, a $750 dress and we may never get there. But the fog lifted and we eventually arrived in London.

I went to the theater for rehearsals. As the show's producer, Lord Lew Grade, was giving out our stage directions, I asked him when my wife and I would meet the queen.

"Only you get to meet the queen," Lord Grade informed me. "Spouses do not have an audience with her majesty."

So I met the queen backstage before the show. She was predictably reserved and gracious, and she had cue cards telling her who each person was. Meanwhile, Ginnie sat in the audience next to my agent, wearing her $750 dress.

•

I've had the chance to rub elbows with several presidents, but no really funny stories came from those encounters.

I met both Lyndon Johnson and Ronald Reagan in the White House. I met Gerald Ford, neither at the White House nor on the golf course, and I met Bush 41 at a nonpartisan meet-and-greet reception at producer Jerry Weintraub's house. I had a photo op in the Oval Office with Bush 43 when I received the Mark Twain Prize.

I never met JFK, but I campaigned for him because he was Catholic. I'm not sure my priest ever came out and said as much, but everyone knew that unless you helped elect the first Catholic president you would go to hell.

I was also one of the entertainers at JFK's infamous birthday party in June of 1962, the one where Marilyn Monroe sang her breathless version of "Happy Birthday, Mr. President." I didn't actually see that because I performed on closed-circuit TV. I did stay at the Carlyle, JFK's favorite hotel. I didn't, however, bump into him in the lobby.

During Reagan's first term, I performed in the East Room of the White House for a bipartisan governors' conference. Before the performance, Ginnie and I were greeted by Ronnie and Nancy. For about twenty minutes, Ronnie and I exchanged funny stories. A colonel on the White House staff told my road manager that it was very rare for the president to spend so much time talking to a guest. That colonel was Oliver North.

At the governors' event, I performed "Abe Lincoln vs. Madison Avenue." Halfway through the routine, it dawned on me that there were rumors of Lincoln's ghost inhabiting the White House. I also threw in some nonpartisan political jokes, such as: "It's eleven o'clock and you're out of the state, do you know where your lieutenant governor is?"

In my stand-up act, I avoid political jokes. My feeling is that the late-night talk-show hosts will have done a similar joke even better. Also, with political humor in normal circumstances, you split the audience in half.

One exception: Al Gore's secret service code name was . . . Al Gore.

When Jimmy Carter was president, I nearly met him. The Rickleses and my family had a VIP tour of the White House when Jimmy Carter was president. We didn't actually go in the Oval Office, but we looked through the door. Carter's sweater was there, but he wasn't.

•

Don Rickles and I are best friends. I know that might seem strange to those who know Don only by reputation, but *somebody* has to be his friend. Just to make sure I don't forget, Don gave me a doormat that sits just outside the front door of my house. It reads: "The Newharts: The Rickleses' Best Friends."

The beginning of my friendship with Don was a lesson in how a comedian's act can differ from the real-life person.

It was the sixties, and both Don and I were playing Vegas. To be precise, I was in the main room at the Sands, and he was in the lounge at the Sahara. Status is one of the primary differences between the main room and the lounge. The main room is high status, the lounge lower status. I never let Don forget this.

Ginnie opened the local paper and discovered that Don

was in town. She decided to call his wife, Barbara. Though she and Barbara had been friends in the past, they hadn't been in touch for a few years. Ginnie reached her and made plans for us to have dinner with her and Don, and then to see Don's last show, which was at 2:00 A.M.

The four of us ate in the Sahara coffee shop, the only place there was back then. Over dinner, Don was telling us how much he hated being on the road all the time. He painted a bleak, sympathetic picture. Though he lived in Los Angeles, he was constantly in Vegas. Barbara couldn't always make the trip to Vegas, so he was alone much of the time. He loved being a family man, but all the travel got in the way of spending quality time with his daughter, Mindy.

Later, as we were walking in to see Don's third show, Ginnie said to me, "He is one of the sweetest men I have ever met. He is such a family man and his values are so solid."

"Honey," I cautioned her, "his act is a little different than the man you just met."

We sat down, and soon Don walked onstage. When the applause died down, he opened his act with this: "Well, I see that the stammering idiot from Chicago is in the audience tonight with his hooker wife from Bayonne, New Jersey."

•

In its heyday, Las Vegas was the place to perform. I played the Copa Room at the Sands, where the Rat Pack, Steve and Eydie, and Jerry Lewis and Dean Martin all appeared regularly. That was a great room, and it had what was called the "Burma Road," which was an upper section that opened if the room was full. If the Burma Road was open—and it often was—the show was a sell-out.

Tickets to sold-out shows were solid gold because there was still an intimacy. Capacity was 750, even with the Burma Road open; there were no 3,000-seat theaters like there are today. The high rollers always sat in the middle of the front section. You could tell who they were because during the show they would sit there sketching on the napkin and talking to themselves. "Let's see, I can get $50,000 on a second mortgage . . ."

That was the Vegas I liked. You didn't ask the club owners what they did before they got into the casino business. It was a much looser place. When the Rat Pack was in town, you could feel the energy in the air. Everybody was partying, every room was full, and you never knew who you were going to see.

Since then, Vegas's identity has changed a few times. For a while, it became a family vacation destination, sort of a Disneyland with activities for grown-ups, like Celine Dion, Danny Gans, and Clint Holmes. But the hotels found the family thing didn't work, so it's now become "What happens here, stays here." Personally, I don't enjoy the corporateness of it. One of the more gut-wrenching sights I have ever seen in my life was the implosion of the Sands to make room for the Venetian.

In the sixties, through our good friends Moe and Lillyan Lewis, Ginnie and I became friends with Ed Sullivan and his wife, Sylvia. When I was appearing at the Frontier, Ed and Sylvia came to my first show one evening and I introduced them to the audience. After the show, I waited for them to come backstage. It was considered good form for a fellow entertainer to come backstage and tell you that they enjoyed the show, even if they didn't.

Ginnie was with me backstage. We waited and waited, but they didn't show up.

"Did you insult Ed?" she asked me.

"Why would I insult Ed Sullivan?" I said. "I didn't insult him. I said some glowing, nice things about him."

"But he didn't come back."

It was getting close to eleven and the next show was at midnight. I needed to eat between the shows, so I told Ginnie that we couldn't wait any longer. As we were walking through the Frontier to the restaurant, we saw a group of thirty Japanese tourists. In the center was Ed Sullivan, signing autographs.

"So I make that out to . . . Nakoweamaso . . . and how would that be spelled? Naka . . . Nakua . . . Nakit . . . Nakowasowi. . . ."

•

As I said before, ever since I've known Don Rickles, I've taken to calling him Chauncey Gardiner after the character in *Being There*, or sometimes Rain Man, the character portrayed by Dustin Hoffman in the film of the same name, because he's so good at what he does and so bad at everything else. In a night club, he is absolutely in total control. In life, he is not.

Don would go to Toronto to play the Boom Boom Club and ask the bellhop how to get there. The bellhop would say, "It's real easy. You go down three blocks and turn left. Then you go two blocks and you will pass the Paramount

Theater. Then you turn right and walk two more blocks and it's right there."

"Okay," Don would say. "I go down two blocks . . ."

"No . . . you go down three blocks . . ."

". . . and turn right . . ."

"No . . . you turn left . . ."

"Let me see if I've got this. I go down . . ."

With that, the bellhop would volunteer to drive Don to the Boom Boom Club.

If Don can avoid doing something, he will. We were sitting around his den one day when he turned to a comedian named Bobby Ramson. "Bobby," Don said, "you're good at that. Would you open the window?"

Ginnie and I have traveled the world with Don and Barbara Rickles, though you wouldn't know it by looking at the movies from our trips. Because Don didn't know how to operate the video camera, I was always saddled with the job. Consequently, I was never in any of the pictures.

Finally, one year before we headed off to Milan, Barbara interceded. "Donald, you have to learn how to operate the camcorder," she said. "It's not fair that Bob isn't in any of the videos. It's like he wasn't even on the trip with us."

After hiring a guy to come over to his house and demonstrate how to use the camera, Don felt reasonably confident that he could shoot some video. On our first day outside of Milan, we walked to a small village. We happened upon a fountain and decided to videotape ourselves. I reached for the camera, but Barbara insisted that Don was ready. The three of us stood by the fountain, and Don videoed us. Everything seemed to go smoothly. The little red light came on, and we all smiled and waved.

I, for one, was pleasantly surprised. But then on the walk back to the hotel, a thought popped into my head: He didn't turn off the camera. Nah, I told myself, don't be silly. I decided to ask anyway.

"You turned off the camera, right?" I said to Don.

"What?"

"When you finished shooting, you turned off the camera, right Don?"

"Ah, damn it, Newhart," he muttered.

And so to commemorate our trip, we have ten minutes of Don's feet walking down a cobblestone street in Lake Como. In keeping with my perverse sense of humor, I play it as often as I can.

On another trip, the group voted to take a Mediterranean cruise. Actually, the vote was 3–0; I abstained because I wasn't wild about being on a boat. The ship was nice, but it wasn't very big and I didn't know how I would handle the rough water. Nevertheless I was game.

In the planning stages, Ginnie informed me that there was only one penthouse. I told her we should flip for it. No, she said, Don really wants it. Fine, I told her, let him have it.

We boarded the ship and found our staterooms. Ginnie and I had a beautiful room, but it wasn't half the size of the penthouse. But what Don didn't realize was that the anchor was right next to his bedroom window. Every morning on the trip, we pulled into port at 6:00 A.M., and he was awoken by the *clunk, clunk, clunk* of the anchor being lowered.

Don had been in the navy in World War II, and he told me that he was seasick every day. On his ship, they had what were called "running silences," where the seamen were to man their battle stations with minimal noise. But every time they sounded the silent alarm, Don became incredibly nervous at the thought of being attacked by the Japanese. While running to his post as a gunner's mate, he would drop his helmet and it would bounce down the stairs with a *clang, clang, clang*. The rebuke would come from the commanding officer: "Seaman Rickles, are you trying to warn the Japanese?"

With that naval experience under his belt, sailing on a luxury cruise liner was nothing for Don. The Rickleses had once been on a small cruise ship and experienced rough weather, so every time the ship tossed we would consult Don as to how bad the conditions were.

One evening, the ship hit choppy water with twenty-foot swells. Ginnie was having a terrible time getting ready for dinner. She looked liked a Picasso painting, with eyeliner going up her forehead on one side and down her cheek on the other. I went to the bar, where we planned to meet the Rickleses for a drink before dinner.

Ginnie kept calling Barbara and asking her to ask Don if the waves were as high as they had been on a ship they had taken to Russia—a very rocky crossing. Each time Don would say, "Oh, no. This isn't rough at all. That was much rougher." I knew the swells were at least twenty feet because the bartender told me that was the point at which you begin to feel the boat toss. Ginnie called one final time to tell Barbara she was ready and would meet them in the bar.

"We'll meet you in the dining room," Barbara said. "Don isn't feeling all that well."

The great sailor, Seaman Rickles. His shaky entrance into the dining room is one I'll never forget. I only wish I had it on videotape.

CHAPTER FIFTEEN

People I Wish I'd Known

In my lean years of comedy work, I once did a routine on television about a character named Telfer Mook. I made up the name, and I filed it away for further use with others such as Denut Crown, Willard Hackmeister, and Patrick M. Doyle, noted lecturer and author. A month later, I received an angry phone call from a man named Telfer Mook. He was a real person who demanded that I stop making fun of him.

I wouldn't have minded meeting Telfer Mook. For starters, we could've talked about the origin of his first and last names. But he was too upset about being mocked on television to carry on much of a conversation. Truthfully, I wasn't that distraught to have never met him. But there are a handful of people, famous and not, who I wish I met because I love their stories.

Two comedians I wish I'd met are Joe Frisco and Jimmy Edmundson.

Joe Frisco performed the "jazz dance," which was also known as the Jewish Charleston, but he was best known for his stutter. No one ever knew if Joe really stuttered or if it was a comedy device. When people stutter, a lot of times the listener will try to finish the sentence, and get it wrong.

"I am ggggoingg to the bbbbb . . ."

"Burger King?"

". . . aaaathroom."

You're never quite sure where it's going, which is why stuttering works so well in comedy.

Joe used stuttering to great effect in his act, drawing out stories and punch lines. It was particularly convincing because he delivered it with a friendly, gap-toothed smile.

Joe always talked about being broke because he played the horses. Once he told a story about the time he was staying in some flophouse when he ran into a fellow comedian who didn't have a room.

"You can sttttay with me bbbbut you've ggggot to come up the fffffire escape because they'll chchcharge me double," Joe says.

So the guy scales the fire escape and climbs through the window of Joe's room. A few minutes later, the phone rings. The night clerk is calling to tell Joe he's aware that someone is staying with him and that the hotel will have to charge the double-occupancy rate.

"Oooo-kay," Joe says. "But ssssend uuup another GGGGideon Bible."

Joe had a different outlook on the world than most people. One day, he was called in by the IRS because he owed them money.

The IRS officer tells Joe that he has to pay something. "Oooooo-kay," Joe says. "I'll pppppaay ffffive ddddollars a week."

The agent agrees, and Joe leaves the office. In the lobby, he spots a friend of his and asks what the problem is. The guy tells Joe that he owes the government $3,000 in back taxes. Joe instructs the guy to follow him, and he walks back into the agent's office. Pointing to his friend, Joe says, "Pupupuput him ooooon myyyy tab."

Jimmy Edmundson had a very different delivery. He was called Professor Backwards for his ability to instantly say words backward. Jimmy was very cheap. He had this code he worked up with his manager to find out where his next date was and how much money he was being paid. He would call person-to-person and ask for Mr. Swanson. His manager would say, "Mr. Swanson is not here."

Jimmy would ask, "Do you know where I can reach him?"

"Yes, he'll be at the Fontainebleau Hotel the fifth through the eighteenth."

"Do you know what room he'll be staying in?" The room was the money.

"Yes, he's in room five hundred."

Remember, this is all on an officially unconnected person-to-person call.

"Oh. I thought he was going to be staying in room seven-fifty."

"No, as a matter of fact, he's lucky he's not in room two-fifty."

When Jimmy Edmundson died, *Saturday Night Live*

reported that Professor Backwards was killed in a failed burglary. His neighbors ignored pleas of "Pleh! Pleh!"

I can't help myself, but I love that obituary.

•

I would've loved to have had a drink with W. C. Fields. He was one of the those rare legendary characters. Fields was a big drinker and a fallen-away Catholic—his casting director at MGM was always after him to go to church and straighten out.

It seems that every comedian has a story or two about him. My favorite is the one about Fields standing backstage in a vaudeville house waiting for a guy to finish so he could perform. Suddenly, Fields became infuriated. "That guy is doing my act!" As the guy walked offstage, Fields decked him.

A couple of weeks later, Fields was onstage performing. He finished and walked offstage. The same guy came up to Fields and said, "You stole that from me you son-of-a-bitch!" Fields thought for a second and replied, "He's right, I did steal it from him."

Once Fields was called to testify in a civil suit. His attorney went to the judge and explained that Fields was an alcoholic and his body required him to drink. The attorney asked for permission to have an alcoholic beverage in the courtroom. The judge refused, but the attorney persisted. Finally, the judge agreed to let Fields have a pitcher of vodka because it looked like water. The only problem was that every time Fields poured himself another drink, he would hoist his glass in a toast to the judge.

Fields lived on the fairway at the Lakeside Country

Club, or the drinker's golf club for short. Though Fields was a lousy golfer, he supposedly liked living near the grounds because during Prohibition he had crates of booze sent by boat across nearby Toluca Lake.

One afternoon, Fields was sitting in his backyard tipping back a few cocktails when a golf ball sailed in. Two guys soon followed and asked if they could retrieve the ball. Fields obliged and chatted with the men. Feeling magnanimous, Fields asked them if they had any dinner plans. They didn't. Fields insisted they be his guests at Chasen's after they finished their round of golf.

An hour later, the guys appeared at Fields's house. They told him they needed to change clothes first, so Fields volunteered to drive them. Fields followed their directions and ended up in front of a church. Turns out, the guys were priests. They changed into their robes, and Fields drove them to Chasen's.

Fields wasn't much of a religious man. His friend Bill Grady, who was head of casting at MGM, was always after Fields to go with him to church, but Fields always found a reason why he couldn't.

When Fields and the two priests walked into Chasen's, the first person they saw was the MGM casting director who was always trying to convince Fields to find religion. The casting director took one look and said to Fields, "That's about as cheap a stunt as I've ever seen in my life, and you should be ashamed of yourself." Then he turned to the two priests and said, "Neither one of you sons of bitches will ever work in another MGM movie as long as you live."

In his final days, Fields took to reading the Bible. The

story goes that Gene Fowler visited him and asked a de-
vout atheist why he was reading the scriptures. Fields
replied, "I'm looking for a loophole."

•

I met Laurel, but not Hardy. It was 1960, and Oliver Hardy
had already died. I called Stan Laurel and asked if I could
meet him. I had always been a great admirer of their material because it holds up so well. That and it's funny.

Laurel lived on Ocean Avenue in Santa Monica with his
sixth or seventh wife, who was Russian. This was before
the days that six or seven wives was acceptable for performers. He had had a stroke on his right side that wasn't
fatal; Hardy had a stroke on his left side that was.

Laurel's incredible laughter immediately took me back
to my childhood and their routines. Laurel and Hardy's
theory of comedy was tell them what you are going to do,
do it, and then tell them why you did it. I loved how they
constantly broke the fourth wall and talked to the audience. Laurel would turn and say, "Did you see what he
just did?"

I wish I would have met Hardy.

•

In my mind, Peter Sellers was probably the best film comedian ever. He was a complicated man haunted by pow-
erful demons, but he was an absolute comic genius.
Apparently, his gift of mimicry was unsurpassed. He had
an uncanny ability to replicate people he had just met.
Unwittingly, he paid me one of the highest compliments
of my career.

A year or so after my first album came out, I was standing in line at the grocery store, and I bumped into the British actor Graham Stark, who was a friend of Sellers's. Graham introduced himself.

"Peter Sellers is big fan of yours," he told me. "When your record came out, he bought thirty copies and gave them out to the cast and crew of *Dr. Strangelove.*"

When I worked on *In & Out*, Kevin Kline and I used to take turns quoting entire scenes of *Dr. Strangelove* to each other. I've seen the movie at least thirty times. Sellers was extraordinary, playing Strangelove, President Merkin Muffley, and Group Captain Lionel Mandrake. My kids always knew what room I was in because they could hear me laughing hysterically at Peter Sellers in *Dr. Strangelove.*

I met Sellers briefly, but he never mentioned the album.

CHAPTER SIXTEEN

I Don't Know How to End This

My wife came up with one of the most famous endings in television history. We were at Marvin and Barbara Davis's Christmas party when I mentioned to Ginnie that the current sixth season was going to be the final year of *Newhart*.

Newhart began in 1982 when I went to my manager, Artie Price, and told him that I wanted to get back into TV. He told me that was fine, but asked me not to tell anyone. Then he called CBS and said, "I may be able to talk Bob into coming back to TV."

I met with Barry Kemp, who had written for *Taxi*, to kick around ideas for the show. I asked him about the setting. He pictured New England. I told him that I had in mind the Pacific Northwest. "Great," he replied, "we're both thinking America." Of course, we ended up setting the show in the Stratford Inn in Vermont, which seemed like a nice compromise.

We made the most of the setting. I loved the speech in the pilot episode where my character, Dick Loudon, informed a group of ladies from the Daughters of the American Revolution about the truth of the inn. "Ladies, according to my information, in the winter of 1775 when all your ancestors were staying here, the Stratford wasn't so much an inn as it was a house of . . . Let me put it this way—there is every reason to believe that you are not so much daughters of the war for independence as you are daughters of a three-day pass."

Like *The Bob Newhart Show*, *Newhart* was filmed in front of a live audience, and I came out before the show and performed a short warm-up act. Having the audience affected the show greatly. The Darrells, for instance, were supposed to be a small diversion in one episode, but the audience response was so overwhelming that they became recurring characters.

In the episode, I found the body of a witch in the basement of the Stratford, and it freaked out my wife, Joanna, who was played by Mary Frann. The minister, played by my father-in-law, Bill Quinn, told us we had to get rid of the witch because it couldn't be buried in hallowed ground. I went to the telephone book and found an ad that read "Anything for a buck."

Not wanting to scare off the workers, I called and told them we needed some work done in the basement. Larry, the guy who answered, told me that they couldn't possibly get to it until next Thursday. I told him it was urgent, and he asked what it was.

"We have the body of a witch in our basement," I blurted out.

"We'll be right over," he said.

When they arrived, Larry introduced himself, as well as his brother Darrell and his other brother Darrell. The Darrells didn't speak. They were like something out of *Deliverance.* I casually asked Larry how he was doing, and he told me that he had hurt his back last week crawling under a house.

"That sounds like tough work," I said.

"It wasn't work," Larry said. "I just enjoy crawling under houses."

Newhart had great characters and that made the show so much fun. I enjoyed playing Dick Loudon, who was comfortable being a middle-aged man. Dick's dream of writing his books in the picture-perfect Vermont countryside while running an inn had come true. He was earnest, easygoing, and orderly, which made for an amusing combination.

But by the end of the sixth season, I contemplated ending the show because the network was tossing us around the schedule. Contractually, I had the right at the end of six years to pull the plug on the show. After *Newhart* established a beachhead at 9:00 P.M. on Mondays, CBS shifted us to 8:30 and then to 9:30 so it could launch new shows in our successful time slot. I thought it was unfair to the show. We had established 9:00 P.M. as a hit time slot, and they were acting very cavalierly toward a successful show. Nobody seemed to know when we were on—not even us.

By the middle of the eighth season, I was sure it was time to move on.

"When it's the last year," Ginnie had said to me at the Davises' Christmas party, "you ought to end it in a dream sequence where you wake up in bed with Emily and you describe this weird dream you had of this inn you owned in Vermont and the strange people." It was perfect because there were so many inexplicable things in the show: The maid was an heiress, her boyfriend (who became her husband later in the show) talked in alliteration and you couldn't understand him, the handyman missed the point of everything, and there were these three woodsmen, but only one of them talked.

Right away I had known it was a great idea. Coincidentally, Suzanne Pleshette had been at same Christmas party with her husband, Tommy Gallagher. Ginnie had told Suzanne about the ending she had come up with. She thought it was a hysterically funny idea and said, "I'll do it in a New York minute."

Once the writers at *Newhart* started on the episode and began fleshing it out, I worried that the script would somehow be leaked to the press. To combat the problem, we hatched a fake finale and wrote a decoy script. The story was entirely plausible, too. In the episode, Bob gets hit by a golf ball, dies, and goes to heaven. At the pearly gates he is greeted by God—played by George Burns.

Sure enough, a couple of weeks later the *National Enquirer* ran the headline: "Bob Gets Zapped by Golf Ball, Dies and Then Meets . . . God!"

As for the real idea, we didn't tell the cast or the crew. Only the producers, the director, Dick Martin, and myself knew right up until shooting day. I told the cast that morning. Mary Frann was a little upset at the concept, and truthfully, there was some concern about how people would react.

To maintain the surprise until the last minute, we had the old set blocked by a floating set that could be moved on cue so the audience couldn't see it until we were ready. After the crew returned from dinner break, we told them we had added a scene. Dick directed each cameraman where to shoot and told them not to move no matter what happened. Then, we let the audience into the theater.

Dick called "action," and the floating set moved to reveal the original bedroom set from *The Bob Newhart Show* and two bodies in bed. The audience reaction was immediate and the applause and screams rocked Stage 17. They recognized the set from the other show, and they knew where we were going.

"Honey, honey, wake up," Bob Hartley implores Emily. "You won't believe the dream I just had."

Emily switches on the light. "All right, Bob. What is it?"

"I was an innkeeper in this crazy little town in Vermont. The maid was an heiress; her husband talked in alliteration; the handyman kept missing the point of things, and then there were these three woodsmen."

"That settles it," Emily replies. "No more Japanese food before you go to bed."

"I was married to this beautiful blonde. . . ."

"Go back to sleep, Bob," Emily says, switching off her light.

"Good night, Emily," I say, switching off mine.

"What do you mean beautiful blonde?" she says, switching her light back on.

"Go to sleep, Emily. You know, you really should wear more sweaters."

I had people tell me later they were alone in a hotel room watching and they stood up and went, *"Yes! Yes!"*

The show didn't air until three weeks after the taping

date. We sent the tapes to critics with a letter imploring them not to disclose the ending. Amazingly, the secret didn't leak out.

One problem we encountered was that we edited the show down to thirty-five minutes, but we couldn't cut it down any more. We went to CBS and told them about our length dilemma, and they agreed to notify the affiliates that *Newhart* would run thirty-five minutes, instead of the usual thirty.

Unfortunately, some of the stations in the Northeast didn't get the memo, so after thirty minutes, they cut to a commercial. The next day, people were reading in the papers about this wild ending on *Newhart* and they had no idea what the paper was talking about. Their feeling was the ending didn't make any sense; the show just ended. The following week, CBS reran the episode.

The response was overwhelming. More than 30 million viewers tuned in to watch the finale. Over the years, the legend of that episode has only grown.

TV Guide named it one of the five most memorable moments in TV history. *The Egg* gave us an even higher distinction, ranking us third in its 100 most memorable moments on TV. We beat out such classics as Rob Petrie stepping around the ottoman for the first time on *The Dick Van Dyke Show* in October 1964, and Geraldo hosting his eponymous show from a topless donut shop on November 2, 1989.

•

In my career, I've ended two series on my own, and I've been ended the other three times by a collaboration of the American public and the network.

In 1962, I became perhaps the only performer in television history whose show received an Emmy, a Peabody, and a pink slip all in the same year.

Truthfully, that show, the first *Bob Newhart Show,* was borderline. It was a variety show, hosted by me. I was fine in the monologues, which were basically stand-up routines, but turning out one a week was killer given that I had spent a lifetime developing my stage routines. Next would come a musical guest, followed by a series of sketches. I never felt comfortable in the sketches. Consequently, they weren't very good.

(Somewhere just before the 1961–1962 show, Jerry Perenchio was my responsible agent at MCA. Jerry wound up one of the partners in Univision, which is on the block for between $12 and $14 billion. I should have paid more attention to Jerry's investment advice.)

Midway through the first season, I wanted to call the whole thing off. I wasn't getting along with the executive producer, Roland Kibbee. At Christmastime, I returned to Chicago and called my manager, Tweet Hogan. I told Tweet that I was unhappy doing the show and wanted to return to stand-up. I suggested that he call my agents at MCA and have them tell NBC "that Bob doesn't want to do the show" so that the network could move another show into our time slot.

Two days later, Dave Baumgarten, who was a vice president at MCA, flew to Chicago to explain to me that things don't work that way. Because I had a contract, I would be sued by the network. So I returned to the show in the new year. By February, Kibbee had been replaced as executive producer by Ralph Levy, whose background included

The Jack Benny Show, and I had become head writer to exercise more control over the material.

After the first season ended in 1961, we were on the bubble for being canceled. There had been considerable tension between the show and the network the first year, so I wasn't terribly anxious to continue. I met with Mort Werner, who was the head of entertainment for NBC, and he told me that the network wanted to make changes of its own, starting with firing the announcer, Dan Sorkin.

Though I didn't know much about TV, I explained to Werner that Dan was largely responsible for me first becoming noticed by Warner Bros. Records back in Chicago, without which NBC would've never heard of me, so there was no way I would go along with that. He told me that he doubted they would continue with the show. Official notice followed a few months later.

I was both relieved and shaken. I was happy to be returning to stand-up, where I knew what I was doing, but I was also afraid that I was about to be outed as a flash in the pan.

After ending the next two successful series, *The Bob Newhart Show* and *Newhart*, largely on my own terms, I returned to television in *Bob*. It was a mixed-genre show, and I played a cranky (or was it edgy?) comic book artist. We said we were going to give the American public a Bob they had never seen before, and after thirty episodes, we found out that the American public didn't want a Bob they had never seen before.

In 1999, I was asked to return to television again. I was sent a very funny pilot script about a bookstore owner living in Martha's Vineyard whose daughter is marrying into a suspicious Vegas family. I was reluctant to do TV again, so I turned down the script. But Les Moonves, who was head of CBS at the time and is now head of the world, called Artie and asked me to reconsider.

I did, and for my own personal superstitious reasons, they christened the show *George and Leo*, owing, as I mentioned earlier, to my given first name being George. I enjoyed working with Judd Hirsch, who played a small-time Vegas con man named Leo. There were some funny bits, but the show never rose to a consistent level.

My favorite was a scene in the pilot. When a hit man shows up at my house to bump off Leo, a nervous George is running out the door to try and right the situation. "Don't whack anybody till I get back," George says. The network didn't wait long before whacking the show.

Sometimes you have to admit that it's somebody else's turn.

·

The real end, of course, is death. I've been there, too, and not just figuratively onstage. It happened on *ER* when I played a character named Ben Hollander for three episodes in 2003. It was my first intentionally dramatic role on television. I had done other things that were meant to be comedic but turned out tragic. I've never had the Hamlet fixation that comedians typically have, that there is a Hamlet inside you clawing to get out.

When the show's executive producer, John Wells, called me and outlined the part, I was intrigued. The character I played, Ben Hollander, had lost nearly everything in life. His wife had died two years earlier, he was estranged from his daughter, and now he was suffering from macular degeneration, which was taking away his forward-looking eyesight and leaving him unable to paint. I knew I would never contemplate suicide, because I have a wife, kids, and grandchildren. But I understood the character well enough to empathize with him.

While being treated in the E.R., Ben befriends the doctor played by Sherry Stringfield. She agrees to have dinner with him at his house but misses the engagement. That night, he commits suicide.

"Oh, great," Sherry said to me, "I get to be known as the actress who caused Bob Newhart to kill himself."

•

Comedy can help us make it past something very painful, like death. Laughter gives us distance. It allows us to step back from an event over which we have no control, deal with it, and then move on with our lives. It helps distinguish us from animals. No matter what hyenas sound like, they are not actually laughing. It also helps define our sanity. The schizophrenic has no sense of humor. His world is a constantly daunting, unfriendly place. The rational man is able to find humor in his.

I remember when John F. Kennedy was assassinated. I was opening at a theater in the round in Anaheim, California. Dinah Shore was the closing act. We went dark for two nights after the assassination. On the third day, I received a call from Sandy Lewis, the promoter. He asked if I would consider doing a show that night, and I told him that if Dinah would, I would.

I was very apprehensive. The theater was full. I went out and did my act without mentioning the Kennedy assassination. The audience was fantastic. They were one of the most receptive audiences I have ever played to in my life because they were ready to laugh.

That week, one horrendous story after another unfolded. But the audiences kept filling the theater, and they kept laughing. People had to escape from the tragedy. For an hour and a half, they needed to blot out the real world. They were saying, "I'll deal with life when the show's over, but right now I need to laugh."

That's what comedians do. They help people get past pain. I've been asked to help do this by speaking at funerals.

It's not easy speaking at a funeral. I've done it many times. On *The Simpsons*, I spoke at Krusty the Clown's funeral.

In the show, I played myself, albeit drawn by the animators. The script was written by a former *Newhart* writer named David Mirkin.

Anyway, my character was just killing time waiting for a different funeral to start, and I was dragged onstage to eulogize Krusty, whom I didn't know.

"I started my career several years before Krusty . . . so I never really learned anything directly from him. . . . I think in a way, in a meaningful way, all of us have learned from him. . . . That is from him being a clown on television for so many years . . . even though many of us . . . didn't watch his show."

What do you say about someone you don't know? "Everybody seemed to like him. . . . He was a great man, a terrific father, and a credit to his community."

When the actor Dick Crenna died, his wife, Penny, asked me to speak at the funeral. I knew Dick and his sense of humor, and she wanted some comic relief for his friends.

Dick lived in Royal Oaks, a very exclusive neighborhood in the San Fernando Valley. Dick and I belonged to the same country club, which was over the hill in Bel-Air. Here's what I came up with:

"In my life, I've driven to the Valley and back maybe 300 times, and nothing ever happened. But Dick Crenna never made one trip to the Valley and back when something didn't happen to him. He would show up at the club and say, 'Will someone please explain to me why . . .' and then Dick was off on another one of his pet peeves."

You see, it's not easy speaking at a funeral.

•

Here are some of the towns I played last year: Carmel, Indiana; Hutchinson, Kansas; and Huntsville, Alabama. I even played Peoria. So why not limit my dates to easy-to-reach cities like Toronto, Chicago, and Reno? Easier still, why not just retire?

Performing stand-up comedy is a narcotic that I need—even if I only do it a few times a year. All the traveling and taking my shoes off in airports is inconvenient, but to me it's worth it because I can make people laugh. This does do some good. I've noticed that people with a sense of humor tend to be less egocentric and more realistic in their view of the world. They also tend to be more humble in success and less defeated in times of travail.

Humor is also our way of dealing with the inexplicable. We had a major earthquake in Los Angeles in 1994, and it wasn't more than three or four days later that I heard the first earthquake joke. Someone said, "The traffic is stopped, but the freeways are moving."

The alternative to performing was playing golf every day. At one point in my life, I thought I could spend five days a week on the golf course. I even tried it. But it was painful going to the club every day watching everyone's terrible golf shots, not to mention hitting my own terrible golf shots. All that golf also left me with a bad back.

Sure, I could rest on my laurels, but to me that's *Sunset Boulevard.* That's sitting in a darkened room, having Erich Von Stroheim come in and ask me which episode of which version of *Newhart* I'd like to watch that day.

I once asked Billy Crystal—on the golf course, come to think of it—if he was still doing stand-up. He told me that he was getting back into it, trying out some new material. I told him how pleased I was because I think that people who are able do stand-up have an obligation to perform. If you are able to take the stage and make people laugh, then you must oblige. A lot of stand-ups who land movie careers say, "Thank God I don't have to do that anymore." But I really believe that if you have the ability, there is an obligation to make people laugh.

Many years ago, I appeared on *The David Susskind Show.* That particular show featured an hour-long discussion with people like Buddy Hackett, Alan King, and Tom Poston. This was shortly after *The Button-Down Mind* broke, so I had been a working stand-up for about five minutes.

On the air, David asked me if I had a degree. I told him that I graduated from Loyola University with a degree in accounting. Technically, my degree was in "management," but I told him it was in accounting because accounting is funnier than management—whatever that is.

With that, Buddy, in his own inimitable voice, countered with: "You mean, you don't have to do this?"

Truthfully, I did. And I still do.

> > > > > >

MORE ABOUT BOB

Bob Newhart's career has spanned several successful television series, fourteen feature films, and millions of albums sold worldwide. He is the recipient of many honors, including the prestigious Mark Twain Prize for American Humor, presented by the Kennedy Center.

Bob's career began in a quite unassuming fashion, while working as an accountant in Chicago. Bored with his accounting work, Bob would call Ed Gallagher, a friend from a suburban Chicago stock company, and improvise comedy routines. It was suggested that they record and syndicate them. They did, and were immediately unsuccessful. Ed, an advertising executive, was offered a job in New York and accepted it, leaving Bob with the difficult job of going it alone. He knocked around Chicago finding occasional work in voiceovers and commercials while still writing additional material.

Through a friendship with disc jockey Dan Sorkin, Bob met with the head of Warner Bros. Records, who, upon hearing Bob's material, offered him a recording contract. And so *The Button-Down Mind of Bob Newhart* came into being, which became the first comedy album to go to #1 on the *Billboard* charts.

Seven more albums followed, each an extremely successful multi-platinum project. Bob's cumulative recording career earned him three Grammys. His record for holding the number #1 and #2 *Billboard* chart positions was not broken until recently, by the rock band Guns 'N Roses. It is still ranked as the 20th best-selling album of all time, according to *Billboard*.

Bob has enjoyed tremendous success in television and films as well and has hosted the *Tonight Show* 87 times. He earned an Emmy and a Peabody Award for his work on the *Bob Newhart Variety Show*, which was quickly followed by *The Bob Newhart Show* (1972–1978) and *Newhart* (1982–1990). He has appeared in over 14 feature films, including *On a Clear Day You Can See Forever*, *Catch-22*, and *Legally Blonde 2*, and has starred with the likes of Steve McQueen, Bobby Darin, Barbra Streisand, Madeline Kahn, and Walter Matthau. Most recently, he has starred opposite Tom Selleck, Kevin Kline, Will Ferrell, Reese Witherspoon, and Noah Wyle. Bob has also provided character voices for major animated films.

Despite his successful run in television and feature films, Bob has never strayed far from his first love of performing stand-up. Recently, *The Bob Newhart Show* received TV Land's prestigious Icon Award at a gala televised ceremony, and Bob headed back to the small screen on a recurring basis, his first such venture in over a decade.

In 2005, Bob appeared as Morty, the estranged boyfriend of Susan's mom, Sophie (guest star Lesley Ann Warren), on *Desperate Housewives*. He was also recently featured in a TNT original adventure drama, *The Librarian: Quest for the Spear*, filmed on location in Mexico City and also starring Noah Wyle, and has also enjoyed acting turns on the NBC drama *ER*, for which he received an Emmy nomination, and in the feature film *Elf*. A second installment of *The Librarian*, filmed in South Africa, airs in December 2006 on TNT. In July 2005, PBS featured Bob in a one-hour *American Masters* presentation.

Bob has a variety of projects planned for the future, including additional acting roles, Las Vegas shows, a concert tour, and a DVD based on his classic routines, featuring "The Driving Instructor" and "The Nude Police Line-Up." The first season of *The Bob Newhart Show* was released for the first time on DVD in April 2005, followed by seasons two, three, and four.

Among Bob's other honors is his selection as Grand Marshall of the 102nd Tournament of Roses Parade, joining 101 other world-famous leaders, stars, politicians, and other world notables. He has also been inducted into the Academy of Television Arts and Sciences Hall of Fame.

Bob and his wife, Virginia, live in Bel Air, California. They have four children—Rob, Tim, Jennifer, and Courtney—and seven grandchildren.

Visit Bob Newhart online at:
www.bobnewhart.com